OF MICE AND MEN

John Steinbeck

AUTHORED by W.C. Miller
UPDATED AND REVISED by Damien Chazelle

COVER DESIGN by Table XI Partners LLC
COVER PHOTO by Olivia Verma and © 2005 GradeSaver, LLC

BOOK DESIGN by Table XI Partners LLC

Published by GradeSaver LLC, www.gradesaver.com

First published in the United States of America by GradeSaver LLC. 2008

ISBN 978-1-60259-162-2

Printed in the United States of America

For other products and additional information please visit
http://www.gradesaver.com

Table of Contents

Biography of John Steinbeck (1902-1968)......1

About Of Mice and Men......3

Character List......5

Major Themes......9

Glossary of Terms......15

Short Summary......19

Summary and Analysis of Chapter One......21
- Summary......21
- Analysis......22

Summary and Analysis of Chapter Two......25
- Summary......25
- Analysis......26

Summary and Analysis of Chapter Three......29
- Summary......29
- Analysis......30

Summary and Analysis of Chapter Four......33
- Summary......33
- Analysis......34

Summary and Analysis of Chapter Five......37
- Summary......37
- Analysis......38

Summary and Analysis of Chapter Six......41
- Summary......41
- Analysis......41

Suggested Essay Questions......45

The Mentally Impaired in Classic Literature......49

Author of ClassicNote and Sources......51

Table of Contents

Essay: Violence and Sadism in John Steinbeck's Of Mice and Men....................53

Essay: Camaraderie: Deciding an Individual's Fate..57

Quiz 1...59

Quiz 1 Answer Key...65

Quiz 2...67

Quiz 2 Answer Key...73

Quiz 3...75

Quiz 3 Answer Key...81

Quiz 4...83

Quiz 4 Answer Key...89

Biography of John Steinbeck (1902-1968)

John Steinbeck was born in Salinas, California in 1902, and spent most of his life in Monterey County, the setting of much of his fiction. He attended Stanford University intermittently between 1920 and 1926. Steinbeck did not graduate from Stanford, but instead chose to support himself through manual labor while writing. His experiences among the working classes in California lent authenticity to his depiction of the lives of the workers, who remain the central characters of his most important novels.

Steinbeck's first novel, *Cup of Gold*, was published in 1929, and was followed by *The Pastures of Heaven* and, in 1933, *To a God Unknown*. However, his first three novels were unsuccessful both critically and commercially. Steinbeck had his first success with *Tortilla Flat* (1935), an affectionate and gently humorous story about Mexican-Americans. Nevertheless, his subsequent novel, *In Dubious Battle* (1936) was notable for its markedly grim outlook. This novel is a classic account of a strike by agricultural laborers and the pair of Marxist labor organizers who engineer it, and is the first Steinbeck novel to encompass the striking social commentary that characterizes his most notable works. Steinbeck received even greater acclaim for the novella *Of Mice and Men* (1937), a tragic story about the strange, complex bond between two migrant laborers. His crowning achievement, *The Grapes of Wrath*, won Steinbeck a Pulitzer Prize and a National Book Award. It was also adapted into a classic film directed by John Ford that was named one of the American Film Institute's one hundred greatest films. The novel describes the migration of a dispossessed family from the Oklahoma Dust Bowl to California and critiques their subsequent exploitation by a ruthless system of agricultural economics.

After the best-selling success of *The Grapes of Wrath*, Steinbeck went to Mexico to collect marine life with the freelance biologist Edward F. Ricketts, and the two men collaborated on *Sea of Cortez* (1941), a study of the fauna of the Gulf of California. During World War II, Steinbeck wrote some effective pieces of government propaganda, among them *The Moon Is Down* (1942), a novel about Norwegians under the Nazis. He also served as a war correspondent. With the end of World War II and the move from the Great Depression to economic prosperity Steinbeck's work softened somewhat. While still containing the elements of social criticism that marked his earlier work, the three novels Steinbeck published immediately following the war, *Cannery Row* (1945), *The Pearl*, and *The Bus* (both 1947) were more sentimental and relaxed. Steinbeck also contributed to several screenplays. He wrote the original stories for several films, including *Lifeboat* (1944), directed by Alfred Hitchcock, and *A Medal for Benny*, and wrote the screenplay for Elia Kazan's *Viva Zapata!*, a biographical film about Emiliano Zapata, the Mexican peasant who rose to the presidency.

Steinbeck married Carol Henning in 1930 and lived with her in Pacific Grove, California. He spent much of his time in Monterey with his friend, Ricketts, at his

Cannery Row laboratory, an experience which inspired his popular 1945 novel, *Cannery Row*. In 1943, Steinbeck married his second wife, Gwyndolyn Conger, with whom he had two children. 1948 was a particularly bad year for Steinbeck: Ricketts died, and Gwyndolyn left him. However, he found happiness in his 1950 marriage to Elaine Scott, with whom he lived in New York City. Two years later, he published the highly controversial *East of Eden*, the novel he called "the big one," set in the California Salinas Valley.

Steinbeck's later writings were comparatively slight works, but he did make several notable attempts to reassert his stature as a major novelist: *Burning Bright* (1950), *East of Eden* (1952), and *The Winter of Our Discontent* (1961). However, none of these works equaled the critical reputation of his earlier novels. Steinbeck's reputation is dependent primarily on the naturalistic, proletarian-themed novels that he wrote during the Depression. It is in these works that Steinbeck is most effective at building rich, symbolic structures and conveying the archetypal qualities of his characters. Steinbeck received the Nobel Prize for literature in 1962, and died in New York City in 1968.

About Of Mice and Men

John Steinbeck's *Of Mice and Men*, published in 1937, is one of the author's most widely read novels, largely due to its ubiquitous presence in the high school curriculum. As a result, this mythic story of two opposites - the clever, wiry George Milton and the lumbering, powerful Lennie Small - has assumed an important place in the American literary canon. The novel is deceptively simple - it is short and straight-forwardly written. But beneath this approachable surface Steinbeck explores mysterious and haunting themes, largely pivoting on the search for comfort, decency and companionship in a lonely, cruel world.

Of Mice and Men was Steinbeck's seventh novel. Though he had achieved critical and popular success with his two preceding novels, *Tortilla Flat* (1935) and *In Dubious Battle* (1936), *Of Mice and Men* was an instant success on another level altogether. The book was chosen as a Book-of-the-Month club selection and garnered Steinbeck the financial stability and creative confidence necessary for his embarkation on his subsequent novel, *The Grapes of Wrath* (1939), which continues to be viewed as the best work of his career.

Steinbeck drew his inspiration for the work from his experience living and working as a "bindlestiff" - or itinerant farmhand - during the 1920s. In a 1937 interview in *The New York Times*, Steinbeck said that the character of Lennie was based on a mentally impaired man he met in his travels who was prone to episodes of uncontrollable rage. The central question of where or how such a man might fit into society drives the action of *Of Mice and Men*, and the rest of the characters in the book are developed largely in terms of their relationships to this enigmatic central figure.

Steinbeck's novel is not, in the strictest sense, a novel; it's better described as a novelized play. The work is easily divisible into three acts of two scenes each, with each chapter comprising a scene. These chapters all take place in fixed locations. Chapter One occurs, aside from a brief stroll at the very opening, at a clearing by the Salinas River; Chapters Two and Three occur in the bunk house at the ranch where Lennie and George have found work; Chapter Four occurs in the quarters of Crooks, the black stable buck; Chapter Five takes place in the barn; and Chapter Six brings us back to the clearing by the river. In all cases, the introduction and description of characters largely occurs in dialogue rather than in expository prose. With rare exceptions, Steinbeck's narrator is quite unobtrusive. He writes in a combination of stage-directions and dialogue - in other words, *Of Mice and Men* is very much like a play. The Steinbeck critic Susan Shillinglaw describes the work as an experimental "play-novelette, intended to be both a novella and a script for a play."

This play-like structure allowed the work to be quickly adapted to the stage, with the first production mounted on Broadway in 1937, the year of the novel's publication. This production was quite successful, and was directed by the famous playwright

George S. Kaufman. The play was revived in 1974 with James Earl Jones in the role of Lennie. *Of Mice and Men* has also been frequently adapted into cinema - first in 1939, in a production directed by Lewis Milestone (who regularly and skillfully directed adaptations of literary works, including *All Quiet on the Western Front* (1930)), with Lon Chaney, Jr. and Lennie and Burgess Merideth as George. Most recently the novel was adapted in 1992, with Gary Sinise playing George and John Malkovich in the role of Lennie. This version was well-received by critics and regularly supplements high school English class units on the novel.

Character List

George

George Milton. A migrant worker who travels from farm to farm with his mentally impaired friend Lennie during the Depression. The two dream of earning enough money to buy a small farm where Lennie can tend rabbits. By virtue of his mental superiority, George assumes a dominant role with Lennie, acting as a parent. Because Lennie tends to involve George in difficult predicaments, George must be responsible, level-headed and ready to deal with any tragedy that may arise. Despite the many problems that Lennie causes George, he stays with his simple-minded friend as a buffet against loneliness and he retains a palpable hope that the two will eventually leave the aimless life of a migrant worker to live a more fulfilling existence.

Lennie

Lennie Small. A gigantic, mentally disabled man, Lennie is simplistic and docile. He obsesses over simple sensory pleasures, particularly finding great joy in touching soft things, whether a cotton dress or a soft puppy. Although Lennie is inherently innocent, he is still capable of great violence, for he lacks the capacity to control himself physically and has a great protective instinct, especially when it comes to his friend, George. Lennie dreams with George of having a small piece of land; he is obsessed with one aspect of this dream: having a small rabbit hutch where he can tend rabbits. Lennie is incapable of making decisions by himself and relies on George entirely.

Candy

An old, crippled man who has lost his hand, Candy is the swamper at the ranch. He remains attached to his aging dog, who has become so weak and sickly that it depends entirely on Candy to survive. Still, when Carlson objects to the dog's smell, Candy allows Carlson to put the dog out of its misery. Candy is a passive man, unable to take any independent action. Indeed, his one major act in the book - when he offers Lennie and George money in order to buy a piece of land with them - is a means by which he can become dependent on them.

Curley

The son of the ranch owner, Curley is a man of short stature who is nevertheless a formidable boxer. Curley is aggressive, boastful and cocky, with a volatile temper and a tendency to provoke conflict with the weak, as he does with Lennie. Part of Curley's bravado stems from anxiety over his new wife, who everyone widely suspects of being "a tramp." He spends a great deal of time monitoring her, believing her to be off with other men when she is not under his supervision.

Curley's wife

Generally considered to be a tramp by the men at the ranch, Curley's wife is the only major character in *Of Mice and Men* whom Steinbeck does not give a name. She dislikes her husband and feels desperately lonely at the ranch, for she is the only woman and feels isolated from the other men, who openly scorn her. She still holds some small hope of a better life, claiming that she had the chance to become a movie star in Hollywood, but otherwise is a bitter and scornful woman who uses sex to intimidate the workers. Lennie accidentally murders her.

Crooks

The stable buck at the ranch, Crooks is also the only black man in the novel. A proud and bitter man, Crooks has a cynical intelligence and a contemptuous demeanor that he uses to prevent others from inevitably excluding him because of his race. His defensive manner fades, however, once Lennie behaves kindly toward him, and he even considers helping Lennie and Candy with their plan to buy land until the threats by Curley's wife force him back into his normal combative posture.

Carlson

A large, big-stomached man who works at the ranch, Carlson complains about Candy's dog and eventually offers to put the old dog out of its misery. George steals Carlson's gun to shoot Lennie after Curley's wife is murdered.

Slim

The jerkline skinner at the ranch, Slim is a seemingly ageless man who carries himself with great gravity. He gives Lennie one of his new litter of puppies to care for. Curley initially suspects that his wife is having an affair with Slim.

Whit

He is one of the workers at the ranch, a young man who shows Carlson the magazine with the letter from William Tenner.

The Boss

The boss of the ranch is Curley's father. He acts suspiciously of George and Lennie when they arrive, thinking that there's something odd about the two mismatched companions.

Aunt Clara

The woman who raised Lennie. Though deceased, she appears to Lennie in a hallucination when he hides in the brush in Chapter Six. In this hallucination, she appears as a short but hefty woman who berates Lennie for his stupidity.

William Tenner

A former worker at the ranch who drove a cultivator, Whit shows Carlson a magazine that has a letter to the editor that Bill Tenner has written.

Andy Cushman

An acquaintance from grammar school, George tells Lennie that he is now in jail in San Quentin " on account of a tart."

Al Wilts

The deputy sheriff of Soledad. Curley sends Whit to find him when his wife is murdered.

Major Themes

Loneliness of the itinerant worker

If one theme can be thought of as defining the plot and symbolism of *Of Mice and Men*, that theme is loneliness. In many ways, from the outspoken to the subtle (such as Steinbeck's decision to set the novel near Soledad, California, a town name that means "solitude" in Spanish), the presence of loneliness defines the actions of the diverse characters in the book.

The itinerant farm worker of the Great Depression found it nearly impossible to establish a fixed home. These men were forced to wander from ranch to ranch seeking temporary employment, to live in bunk houses with strangers, and to suffer the abuses of arbitrary bosses. George sums up the misery of this situation at several points during his monologues to Lennie - "Guys like us, that work on ranches, are the loneliest guys in the world. They got no family. They don't belong no place" (15).

Of course, as George's monologue puts it, "With [George and Lennie] it ain't like that." He and Lennie have found companionship; they watch out for one another. And beyond that, they have a dream of finding a fixed place they could call home, a farm of their own. They are doing what they can to resist sinking into miserable loneliness, which seems to be the lot of so many other itinerant workers.

This dream, of course, does not come to fruition, and indeed Steinbeck seems to have designed his bleak world to preclude the possibility of escape from the cycles of loneliness and hollow companionship (whether found in drink, in prostitutes, in gambling) that come with financial hardship and dislocation.

Loneliness at home

And it's not just the workers - most of the characters in *Of Mice and Men* exhibit signs of desperate isolation, including those who can be said to have settled into a permanent situation.

Candy, the only other character (aside from Lennie and George) who has an unconditional love for a fellow creature (in Candy's case, his old and feeble dog), is left utterly bereft when Carlson takes his dog out back and shoots it. Candy's immediate attachment to George and Lennie's plan to settle on a farm of their own can be seen as a natural emotional progression following his loss - he looks for new companionship, now that he has lost his poor dog.

Of the other characters, Crooks and Curley's wife also show signs of desperate loneliness, though they respond quite differently. Each is isolated because of special mistreatment. Because Crooks is black, he is shunned by the other men; as we see at the beginning of Chapter Four, he spends his time in his room, alone and bitter. Curley's wife also spends her days hounded by her mean-spirited husband; her attempts to reach out to the other men backfire and win her the (not undeserved) reputation of a flirt.

Both characters, despite their hard and bitter shells, reveal a desire to overcome their loneliness and win friends. Their efforts hinge on Lennie, whose feeble-mindedness renders him unaware of the social stigmas attached to the two. Of course both episodes - Lennie's visit with Crooks in Chapter Four and his talk with Curley's wife in Chapter Five - end (respectively) in bitterness and tragedy. Thus Steinbeck further reinforces the bleakness of life in his fictional world. The one man who could serve as a nonjudgmental companion cannot coexist safely with others.

Alienation from nature

One of the driving forces of discontent in *Of Mice and Men*, and of Lennie and George's dream of securing a farm, is the alienation of the working man from the land. Itinerant workers only fulfill one step in the long chain of tasks leading from planting to harvest - they seed the earth, or they haul in the crop, and then they move on, never establishing a connection with the cycles of the natural world.

George and Lennie's dream of "a few acres" addresses this alienation. They speak of their dream in terms of planting and gardening - they are eager to perform the tasks necessary to live off the land. Their talk about raising cows and drinking their milk, about planting and tending a vegetable garden, contrasts starkly with their actual diet - cans of beans with (if they're lucky) ketchup.

The concept of alienation from nature owes much to the writings of Karl Marx, Friedrich Engels and other communist thinkers. They argued that the rise of industrial economy corresponds to a loss of contact with the natural processes of life. Where a human being was once connected, like the animal he is, to the whole of life (the production of food, shelter, clothing, etc.), in an industrialized world he is reduced to a simple role (lift this hay, sew this hem, rivet this bolt a thousand times) in a larger, bureaucratically-managed workforce. This state of alienation, according to Marx, can fuel a discontent among the workers that leads to revolution. Steinbeck allows us to glimpse at a general malaise that might lead to a "soft revolution" of sorts in Chapter Four, when the outcasts of the ranch fantasize about starting their ranch together. As with most things in this tragic novel, their dreaming comes to naught.

"The Rabbits"

During the novel's opening and closing chapters, Steinbeck describes the activity of the natural world. These passages are rich and interpretable in many directions: it's worth singling out the first of the novel's many allusions to rabbits. Steinbeck writes that the rabbits happily "sit on the sand," and are then disturbed by the arrival of George and Lennie - they "hurr[y] noiselessly for cover" (2). Not until later does this little detail take on a richer significance - rabbits, we learn, represent for Lennie (and George, to a lesser extent) the dream of obtaining a farm of their own and living "off the fatta the lan'" (15). The scattering of the rabbits at the beginning suggests already that this dream will prove elusive.

Because Lennie thinks in concrete terms of his own pleasure, he equates the tending of rabbits - whose soft fur he wishes to pet - with the attainment of utter happiness. Thus he has developed a shorthand for referring to the plan George and he share to start a farm of their own - "I remember about the rabbits" (5). Lennie takes deep pride in the notion that he would be entrusted to raise the rabbits, to protect them, to feed them out of their alfalfa patch. He places the entirety of his future happiness on this one image of caring for rabbits.

This dream of the rabbits becomes literally a dream at the end of the novel, when Lennie hallucinates a giant rabbit who tells him that he will never be allowed to tend rabbits. This highlights the extent to which Lennie bases his entire life around the goal of tending rabbits. Indeed, his only thought after doing something "bad" - whether killing a puppy or killing Curley's wife, all "bad things" seem roughly equivalent in Lennie's mind - is that George will not allow him to tend the rabbits. The manner in which he fails to see his actions in terms of good and evil, and instead views them as good or bad insofar as they are conducive to his ability to pet rabbits, reveals definitively how unfit Lennie is for society.

Women

Of Mice and Men depicts very few women - which shouldn't be surprising considering the characters with whom the novel is concerned. These itinerant laborers don't have an opportunity to settle down with women in mutually respectful relationships, it seems. Instead, they seek the company of prostitutes for "a flop" (57) on the weekends and make due otherwise.

However their attitudes toward women may be tied to their dissatisfying life, the views expressed on the subject have every reason to give the modern reader pause. George expresses respect for only two sorts of women in the novel - on the one hand, the maternal figure represented by Aunt Clara, whose charge to take care of Lennie he has taken on as a responsibility; on the other hand, George respects prostitutes. He says, "Give me a good whore house every time" (61). George likes how straight-forward the arrangement at a house of prostitution is.

The one major female character in the novel, who is not even given a name of her own, does not fit neatly into either category. She is a domestic figure - after all, she is married to Curley and spends most of her time at home - and, at the same time, a flirtatious, highly sexualized figure. Her status, between domesticity and prostitution, makes her extremely problematic in the novel, a source of anxiety and unrest. She leads to trouble, as George immediately observes she will.

A reader might raise an eyebrow at Steinbeck's simple willingness to pin the role of trouble-maker on one unnamed woman. Curley's wife is regularly used as a scapegoat in the novel. She is blamed for the lustful feelings she inspires. Even after she has been tragically killed, Candy shouts misogynist insults at her corpse. Curley's wife's life, clearly, is miserable, yet we are not encouraged to see things from her perspective. Even when she expresses her miserable loneliness, these episodes are followed by instances of manipulation, of threatening. Her death is hardly poignant - and indeed, her corpse is praised more in death than she was in life. The reader has every reason to question Steinbeck's motives in giving us such an unsympathetic view of this woman - and, by association, women in general.

"Handiness" in violence and sex

One of the ways that Steinbeck creates such depth in his novels is that he associates certain images with multiple interpretive dimensions. For instance, "the rabbits" captures Lennie's innocent love of tactile stimulation, his participation in George's dream of establishing a farm of their own, and the threat of his daunting strength. Every cuddly thing he's touched, after all, has died - just as the dream of the rabbits dies.

Another such image, though perhaps less obvious, is that of hands. Steinbeck speaks of hands regularly in *Of Mice and Men*, most often associating them with the common dualism of sex and violence. The image hinges on the character of Curley - a man both outspokenly pugnacious and lecherous. In the description immediately following Curley's first entrance, he is described as "handy" (29). The term, in this first context, makes reference to his eagerness and ability to fight. He is handy with his fists, so to speak.

Later in the same conversation we hear of a second association with Curley's hands. Candy says that he wears one glove "fulla vaseline" and adds, "Curley says he's keepin' that hand soft for his wife" (30). Thus Curley's hands are tied to sex as well as violence. He fights with the one hand and keeps the other hand soft.

Thus, with this association in place, it's clear why Curley is so humiliated following his fight with Lennie. Lennie crushes his hand, which thus symbolizes not only his loss in terms of fighting ability, but also in terms of sexual power. Lennie proves the better man in both senses. The defeat is thus a symbolic castration of sorts. This symbolism is reinforced when Curley's wife appears to find the big man's defeat of her husband alluring - "I like machines" (88). Of course, Lennie has no idea that he is causing such problems in the realms of sex and violence - he cannot understand these concepts himself. But this only reinforces the sense that such a dangerous, potent, unreflective man cannot continue to operate in the company of others.

Meanness

In the action and language of the novel, Steinbeck explores some of the multiple meanings embedded in the idea of "meanness." First, the word captures the most obvious definition of the term - a "mean" person is, like Curley, petulant, nasty, bullying. Both George and Lennie express their distaste for this sort of man. George says that he "don't like mean little guys" (30). Curley's relish for violence and his constant urge to pick fights contrasts directly with Lennie's comparatively "innocent" violence. After Lennie accidentally kills Curley's wife and buries her in the hay, George notes that Lennie "never done it in meanness" (104). Lennie kills out of cuddling, or blind panic. He loves things to death.

A second resonance in the concept of meanness has to do with Lennie and Curley's respective sizes - Curley is a "mean little guy." The word "mean" can also refer to the average, the petty, the small. Curley, in other words, is small not in size alone, but also in his petty actions. He is of average size and terribly anxious about that. Thus he, the mean one, takes out his frustrations on Lennie, who is anything but average.

Finally, the word captures a related third meaning - that of intentionality. Curley (and others) act with meaning. When Curley gets into a fight, he *means* to get into a fight. His violence is premeditated and calculating. In contrast, Lennie does not really know how to *mean* to do anything. He is, in this sense, a character without personal *meaning*. He cannot think ahead, nor can he learn from his past actions - he is stuck in a constant present (with the childish exception of the dream of the rabbits), petting pretty things as he finds them and obeying orders as he receives them. This third resonance is captured when George tells Lennie not to play with his puppy too much. Lennie replies, "I didn't mean no harm, George. Honest I didn't. I jus' wanted to pet'um a little" (47). Lennie never means to be mean - he never means much at all. This, however, renders him all the more dangerous, given his crushing strength.

Social fitness

One concept that Steinbeck clearly borrows from biology is that of environmental fitness. His characters can be described as fit or unfit for their social roles on the basis of their physical and intellectual abilities.

Candy, for instance, is an aged and hunchbacked man who is thus relegated to a low place in the social hierarchy - he is a swamper. (In contrast, Slim, the most respected and impressive worker on the ranch, is described as "ageless.") Similarly to Candy, Crooks - named for his crooked back - works menial tasks. The relegation of these men to such unrewarding jobs may be cruel, Steinbeck suggests, but so is life. As long as they remain isolated and individualized (rather than collective, where they could find power in numbers), these "sub-par" people are treated disrespectfully.

The same rule applies just as mercilessly to other characters in the novel, animal and human alike. Candy's old dog, for instance, is judged offensive by the more fit members of the bunk house society - Slim and Carlson - and so the dog is killed. Candy can do nothing to stop this; he is weak, and in this world the strong survive. The dog himself is a symbol of the cruel fate that awaits the feeble. His crime is smelling bad, and though there are other solutions to this problem - a bath, a new place to sleep - Carlson insists upon killing him.

Lennie, clearly, is not fit to live in society as it exists in *Of Mice and Men.* His intellectual weakness parallels Candy's physical weakness. He lacks a basic sense of right and wrong, fails to control his dangerous physical power, and cannot look after himself. When, in the end, he is effectively euthanized by George, we see that even his friend and companion has accepted that Lennie, like Candy's dog, is better off dead. Steinbeck invites the reader to have a complex emotional response to this bitter truth. After all, Lennie is quite likable and, when around George, controllable. But this doesn't stop the inevitable, bleak truth of Steinbeck's Darwinian social world - in which the unfit attract scorn, rather than sympathy, for their impairments.

Glossary of Terms

"An' I bet he's eatin' raw eggs and writin' to the patent medicine houses" (36)

A reference to common aphrodisiacs of the time; George sarcastically expresses his disgust at Curley's ostentatious sex life.

"S'pose he took a powder" (78)

"Suppose he got fed up and left"

"two shots of corn" (87)

two glasses of corn whiskey

"You're yella as a frog belly" (68)

"You're a coward."

alfalfa

a wheat-like plant used for animal feed

bindle

a load carried on one's back, a bundle

candy wagon

a bus or truck

cuckoo

insane person

dugs

teats or udders, used in reference to animals

euchre

a card game

flop

sexual intercourse

gingham

a durable cotton material used for aprons

Golden Gloves

boxing tournament

goo-goo

a derogatory term for a reformer, short for "good government" clubbers

graybacks

lice

hame

a sidepiece of a horse's harness

handy

good with the hands, specifically with reference to fighting

hoosegow

prison

jack-pin

a metal pin used to tie down ropes on ships

jackson fork

a mechanical hay fork

jail baits

underage women

jungle-up

to camp outside

kewpie doll lamp

a lamp with a base made from a children's toy

liniment

a soothing or pain-killing liquid used on sore body parts

looloo

an attractive woman

Luger

A pistol popularly associated with use by German forces in the first and second World Wars.

pitchers

"pictures," or movies

rassel

"wrestle," or haul

ringer

in horseshoes, a throw that "rings" (or encircles) the target

San Quentin

a state prison located north of San Francisco

skinner, or muleskinner

a worker who drives mules with a whip

slang

gave birth to

slough

to skin

snooker

a type of billiards

swamper

a helper, so named because he mops the floors

twict

a jab

welter

welterweight, a boxing category

Short Summary

The novel, which takes place during the Great Depression, begins beside the Salinas River near Soledad, California, where two migrant workers, Lennie Small and George Milton, are walking on their way to a nearby ranch. They have recently escaped from a farm near Weed where Lennie, a mentally deficient yet gentle man, was wrongly accused of rape when he touched a woman to feel her soft dress.

As they walk along, George scolds Lennie for playing with a dead mouse and warns him not to speak when they arrive at their new place of employment. When Lennie complains about not having ketchup for the beans they eat for dinner, George becomes angry, telling Lennie that he would be better off if he didn't have to take care of him. After they make up, George repeats to Lennie the details of their dream - that he and Lennie will raise enough money to buy a patch of land, where they will have a small farm with a vegetable patch and a rabbit hutch. The rabbit hutch is the only detail of the plan that Lennie consistently remembers. George tells Lennie that, if he gets into trouble as he did in Weed, he should return to the brush near the river and wait for George to find him.

When George and Lennie reach the bunkhouse at the farm where they will work, an old man named Candy shows them their beds and tells them that the boss was angry that they didn't show up the night before. Soon, the Boss questions George and Lennie. He discovers Lennie's mental impairment and cannot understand why George would travel with him until George lies and says that Lennie is his cousin. After the boss leaves, his son, Curley, enters the bunkhouse. Curley is a short man who hates larger men out of jealousy and insecurity; he has a new wife whom everyone suspects is unfaithful. His wife visits the bunkhouse later that night searching for Curley and flirts with the other men. Later, Curley returns looking for his wife and attempts to start a fight with George.

After a day of work, the men return to the bunkhouse. Slim, whose dog had a new litter of puppies, gives Lennie one of them. George admits to Slim that he and Lennie escaped lynching when Lennie was accused of rape. Carlson complains about Candy's dog, a decrepit and stinking creature. He offers to shoot the dog, and after repeated complaints, Candy relents, despite his obvious wish to keep the dog. George complains about "tarts" such as Curley's Wife, and when the other men suggest that they visit a whorehouse the next night, George says that he prefers the company of whores, since with them there is no chance of danger. When George again tells Lennie the story about the house that they will have, Candy overhears. Candy offers to pool his money with theirs if they'd let him work on their farm. A bit later, Curley searches for his wife once more; he attacks Lennie when he suspects that Lennie is laughing at him. Curley punches Lennie several times, but Lennie does not fight back until George gives him permission, at which point Lennie crushes Curley's hand.

While the other men are at the whorehouse, Lennie visits Crooks, the black stable buck. Crooks is rude and contemptuous toward Lennie until he realizes that Lennie has no ill intent. Candy also visits the two men, for they are the only ones left at the ranch while they others are in town. They discuss the plan for a small farm and Crooks shows some interest in joining them. Curley's wife sees the three men and seeks their company out of loneliness; when Crooks tells her that she is not supposed to be in his room, she upbraids them as useless cripples and even threatens Crooks with lynching.

The next morning, Lennie accidentally kills his new puppy when he bounces it too hard. Curley's wife finds him in the barn with the dead puppy. She pities him and allows him to feel how soft her hair is. When he handles her too forcefully, she screams. Lennie covers her mouth and accidentally snaps her neck. After this killing, Lennie flees from the ranch. Candy and George find the body and infer Lennie's guilt. Candy alerts the other men, and Curley forms a party to search for Lennie and kill him. In the interim, George steals Carlson's gun, leading the other men to think that Lennie took it before he escaped.

George, who points Curley and the other men in the wrong direction, finds Lennie in the brush where he told him to return at the beginning of the novel. Lennie has been having hallucinations of a giant rabbit and his Aunt Clara; they warn Lennie that George will be angry at him for killing Curley's wife and that he has lost the possibility of having a house with a rabbit hutch. George reassures Lennie that they will have the rabbit hutch after all, meanwhile preparing to shoot his friend with Carlson's gun. Upon hearing the shot, the other men find George and Lennie. George tells them that Lennie had stolen the gun and that he shot Lennie after the gun got loose in a struggle.

Summary and Analysis of Chapter One

Summary

George and Lennie, two migrant workers during the Great Depression, walk along a trail on the Salinas River just south of Soledad, California. They are on their way to a new ranch, where they hope to be hired to "buck barley," that is, to haul sacks full of grain. A bus driver recently let them out and told them the ranch was nearby. However, the walk is much longer than they anticipated.

George is a small, quick man with dark, suspicious eyes. Lennie is just the opposite: a naive, unintelligent mountain of a man. As they walk along, Lennie comes upon a pool of water and drinks thirstily; George warns him that the water might be bad as it has been stagnant in the sun, but Lennie pays him no heed. After Lennie drinks his fill, George quizzes him on the upcoming job. Lennie, however, fails to remember even the slightest detail of their current prospect. George reminds him that they have received work cards from Murray and Ready's.

As George pats his pocket, where the work cards are kept, he notices that Lennie has something in his pocket as well: a dead mouse. Lennie explains that he likes to pet the mouse's soft fur as he walks. George takes the mouse from Lennie and throws it into the bushes. He then admonishes Lennie for his behavior, warning him not to behave badly, as he has done so often in the past, and ordering him not to say a word when they meet the boss at the new ranch. He reminds Lennie of past misadventures, specifically an episode in the town of Weed in which Lennie assaulted a woman in a red dress because he thought her dress was pretty and wanted to feel it. The woman accused Lennie of attempting to rape her and George and Lennie had to run for their lives out of town. While recounting this incident, George complains that if he didn't have to take care of Lennie he could live a normal life: "I could live so easy and maybe have a girl" (7).

George tells Lennie that they are going to bivouac a couple of miles away from the ranch so that they won't have to work the morning shift the next day. They set up camp and George sends Lennie off to look for firewood so that they can heat up some beans. Lennie goes off into the darkness and returns in a moment; George instantly knows from Lennie's wet feet that he has retrieved the dead mouse. He takes it from Lennie, who begins to whimper. George assures Lennie that he'll let him pet a "fresh" mouse, just not a rotten one. They recall that Lennie's Aunt Clara, whom Lennie refers to as "a lady," used to give Lennie mice to play with.

Lennie fetches some wood and George heats up their beans. Lennie complains that they don't have ketchup, which sets George off on a rant about having to care for Lennie. After this outburst, George feels ashamed. Lennie apologizes and George admits that he's "been mean" (14). Lennie passive-aggressively offers to go away and live in a cave so that George can have fun. George resolves this short argument by agreeing to Lennie's request to "tell about the rabbits," which is Lennie's shorthand for "talk about how things will be for us in the future." George paints a picture of the future – a picture he has obviously painted countless times before – in which he and Lennie have their own place on their own farm and "live off the fat of the land." He promises Lennie that they will have rabbit cages and that Lennie will be allowed to tend them. Lennie repeatedly interrupts George as he tells this story, but insists that George finish it to the end.

As they prepare to sleep, George reminds Lennie not to say a word during their interview with the boss the following day. He also tells Lennie that if he runs into trouble, as he has so many times before, he is to return to the place where they've camped, hide in the brush and wait for George.

Analysis

John Steinbeck's enduring popularity is largely the result of his ability to weave a complicated fictional reality from simple elements – simple language, simple characters, simple techniques. One of the techniques he uses consistently is the juxtaposition of the human and the natural worlds. He often – as in *The Grapes of Wrath* – alternates short natural vignettes with the parallel struggles of humankind. *Of Mice and Men*, as is clear from the title alone, features this parallelism as well. It is a novel about the natural world – "of mice" – and the social world – "and men." The relationship between these two worlds is not one of conflict but of comparison; he invites us to witness the similarities between the human and animal worlds.

The title, *Of Mice and Men*, comes from an eighteenth-century poem by Robert Burns entitled "To a Mouse." This poem features a couplet that has become widely known and quoted: "The best laid schemes of mice and men / Gang oft aglay." That last phrase, written in Scottish dialect, translates as "often go wrong." As will become clear, the quotation relates directly to our two protagonists, who do indeed have a "scheme" to get out of the cycle of poverty and alienation that is the migrant worker's lot: they plan to purchase a farm of their own and work on it themselves. Lennie visualizes this future possibility as near to heaven – he can imagine nothing better than life with "the rabbits." Their action in the novel is largely motivated by a desire to achieve the independence of this farm life.

Poverty, in Burns' work as well as Steinbeck, draws the human and the natural worlds closer together. During the Great Depression, in which the novel is set, workers were thrust from relative comfort to fend for themselves in a cruel and uncaring world. They face the original challenges of nature – to feed themselves, to fight for their stake. Poverty has reduced them to animals – Lennie a ponderous, powerful, imbecilic bear; George a quiet, scheming, scrappy rodent of a man. Notice how frequently the two men, particularly Lennie, are described in animal similes: Lennie drags his feet "the way a bear drags his paws" (2) and drinks from the pool "like a horse" (3). Lennie even fantasizes about living in a cave like a bear.

Of course, Lennie's vision of nature is hardly realistic; he thinks of nature as full of fluffy and cute playthings. He has no notion of the darkness in the natural world, the competition and the cruelty. He wouldn't have the faintest notion how to feed himself without George. In this too the men balance each other: George sees the world through suspicious eyes. He sees only the darkness where Lennie sees only the light. George may complain about how burdensome it is to care for Lennie, but this complaint seems to ring hollow: in truth, George needs Lennie's innocence as much as Lennie needs George's experience. They compliment each other, complete each other. Together, they are more than the solitary and miserable nobodies making their migrant wages during the Depression. Together, they have hope and solidarity.

George's complaint – "Life would be so easy without Lennie" – and Lennie's counter-complaint – "I could just live in a cave and leave George alone" – are not really sincere. They are staged, hollow threats, like the threats of parents and children ("I'll pull this car over right now, mister!"). Similarly, George's story about how "things are going to be," with rabbits and a vegetable garden and the fat of the land, also has a formulaic quality, like a child's bedtime story. Children (like Lennie) love to hear the same tale repeated countless times; even when they have the story memorized, they love to talk along, anticipating the major turns in the story and correcting their parents if they leave out any details. "The rabbits" is Lennie's bedtime story, and while George isn't exactly a parent to Lennie, he is nevertheless parental. George is Lennie's guardian – and in guarding Lennie, George is in effect guarding innocence itself.

Steinbeck's plots are as simple and finely honed as his characters. Each topic discussed - the woman who mistakenly thought that Lennie was trying to rape her, the mice that Lennie crushes with affection, George's order that Lennie return to the campsite if anything goes wrong - will come into play in the chapters to come. Keep these details in mind as we continue.

Summary and Analysis of Chapter Two

Summary

The following morning, George and Lennie reach the bunk house at the farm. Candy, the old man who shows them the bunk house, tells them that his boss was expecting them the night before and was angry when they weren't ready for work in the morning. Near his bed George finds a can of insect poison, which leads him to think that his bunk is infected, but the old man reassures him, telling him that person who had the bed before was a meticulous blacksmith named Whitey who kept the insect killer around even though there were no insects to kill.

As George prepares to meet the boss, Candy reports that he is a nice enough man although he takes his anger out on the black stable buck, Crooks. Soon enough, the boss enters and asks George and Lennie for their work slips. George attempts to speak for both Lennie and himself, but the boss notices Lennie's silence and questions him directly. Lennie attempts to speak for himself, aping phrases that George has spoken, but sounds completely ridiculous. George tells the boss that Lennie isn't bright, but that he's as strong as a bull and an incredibly hard worker.

The boss wonders why George is willing to take care of Lennie; George tells the boss that Lennie is his cousin and that he promised his mother to look after him. When the boss wonders why they left their last job, George tells him that they were digging a cesspool and completed the work. When the boss leaves, George scolds Lennie for failing to keep completely silent. George admits that he lied about Lennie being his cousin.

Candy returns with his old sheepdog, and George snaps at him for eavesdropping. Curley, a haughty young man, enters the bunk looking for the boss, who is his father. He behaves threateningly to Lennie. When he leaves, Candy explains that Curley, who is short, hates big guys like Lennie out of jealousy. George says that however tough Curley may be, he will be sorry if he picks a fight with Lennie, who is incredibly strong. Candy notes that Curley was recently married to a local beauty and that he has become more cocky ever since. Curley wears a left glove full of Vaseline to keep the hand soft for his wife, whom the old man thinks is a tart. George warns Lennie to avoid Curley.

On cue, Curley's wife comes to the bunk house looking for her husband. She is provocatively dressed and quite flirtatious. When she leaves, George remarks that she's a tramp, while Lennie says that she's pretty. George warns him to keep away from her.

Next to enter is Slim, the widely respected jerkline skinner. Slim questions George and Lennie about what work they can do. Carlson, a large, big-stomached man, also enters the bunk house and asks Slim whether his dog had her litter last night. Slim tells him that she had nine puppies, but that he drowned four immediately since she couldn't feed so many. Carlson complains about the smell of Candy's old sheepdog and tells Slim that Candy should put it out of its misery.

Curley enters again and confronts George, asking if his wife has been around. George admits that she was at the bunk house. Curley seems eager to start a fight with anyone.

Analysis

The novel as a whole, and this chapter in particular, shares many elements with stage drama. Steinbeck often uses a single room as a setting for a scene, as the bunk house is used here. This technique allows him to introduce a wide variety of characters quickly without using a narrator - the characters talk about each other, interact, and even describe each other (as when Candy talks about Curley being a "little guy"), all of which facilitates relatively rich characterization in a relatively short number of pages.

This stage technique applies to Steinbeck's descriptions as well as his dialogue. Consider the description of Candy's dog at the close of the chapter: "[The dog] gazed about with mild, half-blind eyes. He sniffed, and then lay down and put his head between his paws [etc.]." Steinbeck's language is completely shorn of emotion; he simply describes the animal's actions as a playwright might write stage directions.

This "dramatic" technique gives Steinbeck's story a portentous quality. On one level, he is simply describing an evening among itinerant workers in a realistic way; on another level, the actions and personae of these workers take on a larger, almost mythic significance. Just as in dramatic works of the same period - such as Thornton Wilder's *Our Town* - Steinbeck blends the workaday with the highly stylized, bringing out the eternal, allegorical character of everyday life. Thus Curley comes to represent all petty, embittered men; Crooks stands in for the persecution and the suffering of all African Americans; George is the eternal cynic-with-a-heart-of-gold and Lennie personifies clumsy innocence. The characters are types, or even archetypes, as much as they are individuals - a technique more popularly associated with plays and films than with literary fiction.

This stage technique also allows Steinbeck to build tension quickly without exposition. The atmosphere of Chapter Two is immediately hostile and uncomfortable: George suspects that his bed is infested, the Boss suspects that George and Lennie are trying to pull a fast one, Candy is miserable and decrepit, Curley is looking for a fight, Curley's wife is vamping around suspiciously. Lennie, in his instinctive, animalistic way, captures the foreboding tone of the Chapter when he bursts out, "I don't like this place, George. This ain't no good place." Right away, there are several points of inevitable conflict, most of them hinging on the character of Curley, who seems to rub everyone the wrong way. The only positive character in the Chapter is Slim, who is also the character described at greatest length; but even

Slim comes off as life-hardened - the first fact we learn about him is that he has drowned four out of his nine new puppies. One should immediately recognize how completely out-of-place Lennie is in this hostile, gloomy environment: he is innocent, naive, clumsy and childish in the midst of a bunch of shrewd, ugly, lonely, conniving men.

And Steinbeck's novel certainly features *men* rather than women. The only woman with any important role in the novel (aside from the memory of Lennie's Aunt Clara) is Curley's Wife, a lonely and desperate "tramp," to use Candy's word, who is every bit as meddlesome as Curley fears. Steinbeck's attitude toward her, at least at this stage in the novel, is hardly sympathetic. She doesn't even receive a name, she dresses garishly and talks provocatively. There is more than a whiff of sexism in her depiction. However, Steinbeck is careful to hint as a possible motive for her behavior even at this early stage. She is, after all, stuck with the most loathsome imaginable husband, Curley - who apparently keeps her confined in their house whenever possible, who obnoxiously brags about their sex life (exemplified by the grotesque image of the Vaseline-filled glove), and who cannot be good company. Curley married her because she was flashy, and now her flashiness causes him nothing but distress. She is stuck in a loveless - and perhaps, despite Curley's bragging to the contrary, a sexless - marriage, and can be pitied for seeking other company.

Speaking of the Vaseline-filled glove, pay attention to how often and how variedly Steinbeck references hands in this Chapter and throughout the book. On the most basic level, hands are crucial to the work of the farm - these men, after all, live by their labor. They also function metaphorically. Curley, especially, is repeatedly described as "handy," a term that Candy uses to mean "good at fighting." His hands are further connected to his sex life - his Vaseline-filled glove creates an association between his hand and his sexual organ (why else, after all, would one soften up one's hand?). This association becomes especially important as the tension established in this Chapter spills over into crisis in the pages ahead.

Summary and Analysis of Chapter Three

Summary

Chapter Three opens on the next day. After working hours, as the other men play horseshoes outside, Slim and George return to the bunk house. We learn that Slim has allowed Lennie to have one of his puppies. Slim praises Lennie for his incredible work ethic, which leads George to talk about his past with Lennie. The two grew up as neighbors and George took Lennie as a travel and work companion when Lennie's Aunt Clara died. George says that when he first began traveling with Lennie he found it funny to play pranks on him. One day he ordered Lennie to jump in a river even though he couldn't swim and Lennie unthinkingly obeyed. After George fished him out, Lennie was completely grateful, having forgotten that George had ordered him into the river in the first place. After this episode, George decided against having fun at Lennie's expense.

At Slim's insistence, George tells about the episode in Weed that led them to seek work elsewhere. Lennie saw a woman in a red dress and, overcome by an urge to feel the pretty fabric, he stupidly grabbed the woman. The woman fled and told the men of Weed that Lennie had raped her. George and Lennie were forced to hide from a lynch mob and sneak out of Weed under cover of night.

Lennie appears with his new puppy and George tells him to take the puppy back to its mother for its own safety. After Lennie leaves, the men come in from their horseshoe game, which Crooks has apparently won. Carlson begins complaining again about the smell of Candy's old dog. He goads Candy to shoot the dog, which Candy refuses to do. Carlson then offers to shoot the dog himself. After Slim speaks up in favor of shooting the dog, Candy reluctantly allows Carlson to take the dog outside with his Luger and a shovel. Candy sinks into a deep melancholy and the men try to lighten the atmosphere with talk of cards and magazine articles. Just as they begin a game of euchre, a shot rings out in the night.

Crooks enters and talks with Slim about fixing a mule's hoof. He also mentions that Lennie is playing with the pups in the barn. Slim leaves for the barn as George and Whit begin a conversation about women. Whit mentions that the men usually go to a whorehouse or two on the weekend and they welcome George to come along. Whit also laughs about Curley's trouble keeping tabs on his wife, who appears eager to spend time with every man on the ranch aside from her husband. On cue, Curley bursts in to the bunkhouse and demands to know the whereabouts of his wife and Slim. After he learns that Slim is in the barn he leaves. Lennie, at the same time, returns from the barn, having been told to stop playing with the pups for the night.

As they wind down for the evening, Lennie asks George to tell him "about the rabbits," and George launches into his monologue about their proposed self-sustaining farm - complete with rabbits, pigs, cats and a vegetable garden.

Candy, who has been listening in, asks how much such a place would cost. George, though put off at first by Candy's nosiness, eventually lets on that he has a lead on a plot of land that could be bought for six hundred dollars. Candy reveals that he has a secret stash of money - three-hundred and fifty dollars - and offers to give it all to George and Lennie if they'll let him live on their farm and work as a housekeeper. After a quick calculation George figures that they could make a down payment on the property after only a month's work. The three men sit, enraptured and astounded that their dream of a self-sufficient farm life might actually become a reality.

Curley returns with Whit, Carlson and Slim. Curley has accused Slim of eying his wife, a charge which Slim and the others laugh off. Lennie, who is still dreaming about the rabbits, also smiles, which leads Curley to confront him aggressively. Curley punches Lennie in the face. Lennie does not immediately fight back, instead crying and calling to George for help. When Curley doesn't back off, George tells Lennie to "get 'em." Lennie catches Curley's next punch in his massive paw and crushes down on his hand. George tells Lennie to let go, but Lennie only grips harder out of fear. Curley flops like a fish. By the time Lennie finally relaxes his grip, Curley's hand has been ruined. Before Curley goes to the hospital, he agrees to pretend that he has caught his hand in a machine. Lennie is afraid that he has done something bad, but George reassures him that he hasn't as the chapter closes.

Analysis

Once again, every visible action in this chapter takes place in the bunk house as characters make their exits and entrances. Steinbeck carefully controls the events, weaving even the smallest detail into a rich whole. The atmosphere remains gloomy as the action progresses from the account of Lennie and George's near-lynching, to the shooting of Candy's dog, to the fight between Curley and Lennie - with one exceptional spot of light, George's monologue "about the rabbits" and Candy's offer to finance their dream.

To take these events as they occur, the near-lynching in Weed provides another instance of the danger of women. Again, Steinbeck gives voice to attitudes that are sexist at best. He already showed Curley's wife acting just as desperately vampy as her reputation; here he piles on examples of the danger and misunderstanding that comes from sex. The woman in the red dress in Weed (whose pretty dress "provokes" Lennie into action) clearly resembles Curley's garishly attired wife. And George tells of another man, Andy Cushman, who landed in the San Quention penitentiary after succumbing to "a tart" (62). Women equal danger in Steinbeck's masculine dramatic world.

The only good women, George suggests (61), are those whose sexual motives one knows - either because they are totally desexualized, like Lennie's Aunt Clara, or completely sexualized, like the whores at Susy's and Clara's. Indeed, Steinbeck's double use of the name "Clara" (which means "clear," suggesting that the social and sexual roles of these two women are transparent) links the one model of womanhood

- motherliness - with its opposite - whoredom. Figures like the woman in the red dress, or Curley's wife, who seem to exist between these two extremes, at once off-limits and up-for-grabs, are presented as dangerous, especially for a man as sexually innocent yet powerful as Lennie. He is as dangerous to them as they are to him - they are like the pet mice and rabbits that Lennie loves literally to death, soft and easily crushed. (Steinbeck heightens the association between the women and the small cuddly creatures at several points, for instance when he writes that the woman in the red dress "rabbit[ed]" to the lawmen with her accusation of Lennie (46).) Readers can certainly take issue with Steinbeck's depiction of women, but their role in the work as kindling for trouble seems quite clear.

The shooting of Candy's dog draws a parallel between the old swamper and George and Lennie. Indeed, Candy and his dog come off as an "old timer" version of the younger duo. Just as Lennie is an incredible worker, so too Candy's dog was once "the best damn sheep dog I ever saw" (49). And just as the other men cannot understand the bond that keeps an apparently hale and clever man like George yoked to the burdensome, infantile Lennie, so too the men cannot understand Candy's sentimental companionship with his now-decrepit and stinking dog. Steinbeck strengthens their parallel bonds of companionship with continued associations of Lennie and dogs - he is absolutely attached to his puppy; he obeys George's commands unthinkingly, as a dog obeys an owner; and George's commands often directly resemble commands one gives a dog, such as when he sics George on Curley.

Candy thus emerges as the only character in the bunk house who has something approaching George and Lennie's preference for social (and perhaps socialist) companionship over isolated individualism. Their thematic link makes his eagerness to join George and Lennie in their farm life natural and understandable. Candy, unlike the others, displays an interest in others and hope for the future. His sympathetic nature comes through even in his decision to allow his dog's death. Candy only relents to their request to put the dog out of its misery when they frame the argument in terms of the dog's suffering, and even this request is not granted easily.

Yet Candy does finally relent to the men, for despite his similarities to George and Lennie, Candy is an inherently passive character. He relents to others' decisions easily, incapable of fully standing up for his own beliefs. He allows another man to shoot his dog, despite his repeated insistence that he wants to keep the old hound. (The shooting of the dog in the back of the head, a supposedly painless maneuver, foreshadows later events in the story.)

The tragic fate of Candy's dog reminds us that the rest of the bunk house society - including even Slim - cannot understand or tolerate sentimental attachment to a weak creature. This is no world for Candy's dog, and it appears to be no world for Lennie either. Steinbeck even subtly suggests that their now-realistic dream of co-owning a plot of land might also be too dreamy for the hard truths of the world. When Candy decides to collaborate with them and the idea of owning a farm becomes tangible, none of the men know how to respond. For George and Lennie their dream serves as a diversion from the travails of everyday life and not as a realistic goal.

To turn to the final episode in the chapter, the fight between Lennie and Curley, we see first-hand that there is a deep and ruthless capacity for violence in the generally docile Lennie. This violence is sometimes casual and inadvertent - as in his accidental killing of the mice in his pockets - and sometimes an explosion of directed rage, as when he crushes Curley's hand. Lennie seems willing to kill to protect the things he loves, whether George or the rabbits or what have you. His violence is child-like - or dog-like: the sudden ferocity of an otherwise affectionate pet. His casual declaration that he will snap the necks of any cats who attempt to kill the rabbits on his fantasy farm is shocking - we know that he means exactly what he says.

When George gives him permission to fight back against Curley, Lennie cannot control his capacity for violence. He only stops crushing Curley's hand when George issues a direct order - leading one to wonder how he would behave in a similar situation is George were not there to control him. The fight between Curley and Lennie fulfills the foreshadowed confrontation between the two characters, but it does not resolve the situation. We know Curley well enough to sense that his spoken resolution to pretend the incident didn't happen - to pretend he caught his hand in "a machine" - rings hollow.

By the way, Lennie's crushing of Curley's hand - an unusual form of fighting, to say the least - is highly significant. We've already seen how Curley's hand is associated with his sexuality - he keeps one hand soft for his wife. Thus the injury he sustains resonates with his (already uneasy) sense of sexual prowess. Lennie has, metaphorically at least, crushed more than the man's hand - he has also crushed his very manhood. Lennie cannot understand the significance of this gesture, but the others - or, at least, the reader - can. Lennie has unwittingly unmanned his rival and indirectly revealed his superior physical (and sexual) prowess. Thus Steinbeck lays the foundation for a conflict that directly links Lennie, Curley, and Curley's sexual object, his wife.

Summary and Analysis of Chapter Four

Summary

This chapter takes place the next night, while all of the men are off at the whorehouse spending their weeks' pay except for the feeble threesome of Crooks, Candy and Lennie. The setting is the "little shed that leaned off the wall of the barn" (73) that makes up Crooks' quarters. Steinbeck gives us a glimpse at the quiet, neat, lonesome life of the black stable buck. While Crooks is belittled and ordered around in the ranch at large, in his bunk he is sovereign; none of the other workers impede upon his living space.

Lennie, however, doesn't understand the unwritten code of racial segregation. He appears in Crooks' doorway while checking on his pup in the barn. Crooks tells Lennie to go away, but the simple big man cannot understand that he isn't wanted. Crooks at last relents and allows Lennie to sit with him and talk. Lennie tells Crooks "about the rabbits" and Crooks vents about his mistreatment as an African-American. Their conversation takes an unsettling turn as Crooks teases Lennie about his lack of self-reliance; he tauntingly asks Lennie what he would do if George were injured. Unable to think hypothetically, Lennie thinks that George is actually under threat. With some difficulty, Crooks calms Lennie down and takes on a kindlier demeanor. His sour attitude remains, however, as he tells Lennie that his dreams of owning a farm with rabbits is unlikely to amount to anything tangible.

Candy comes by looking for Lennie and Crooks is secretly pleased that after so many years of solitude he is finally part of a sort of social gathering. They continue to discuss their plan to buy a farm and Crooks begins to warm to the scheme, even offering his own money and services if they'll take him on as well.

Just as they reach the height of enthusiasm for the plan, Curley's wife enters, ostensibly looking for Curley. She insults the men, noting their feebleness. This offends the two mentally sound farmhands but Lennie finds her fascinating. She voices her frustration at having no one to talk to and launches into a speech about how she could have been a movie star if she hadn't met Curley. She clearly dislikes Curley and tells the men that she knows he was beaten in a fight - that his injured hand did not result from a machine accident. Lennie eagerly tells her "about the rabbits" and she dismisses their plan as a pipe-dream. As he talks, though, she notices the bruises on his face and deduces his role in Curley's injury. She flirtatiously congratulates Lennie on bringing Curley down a notch and Lennie grows increasingly enamored with her beauty.

Crooks sharply tells her to leave and Curley's wife turns on him viciously, reminding him that at any time she could accuse him of raping her, which would lead to his death. Crooks and Candy silently tolerate her superiority until Candy hears the sound of the men returning, which leads Curley's wife to slip away back to her house. Soon

George arrives looking for Lennie; he admonishes Candy for talking about the plan to buy the farm. Crooks assures them, however, that he doesn't really want to be a part of their plan after all.

Analysis

Steinbeck has already implicitly contrasted the lonesome, individualistic existence of most of the farmhands with the more collective, communal attitude of George, Lennie and Candy. In Chapter Four, this contrast becomes still more marked. Indeed, as Crooks, Candy and Lennie - the three mentally or physically impaired "outcasts" of the farm - discuss their dream of living "of the fat of the land" one can sense a strong whiff of socialism. For a moment, they imagine a life of freedom from prejudice and racism, in which each man works for "just his keep" regardless of color or disability (84).

It's fitting that the three virtual servants of the farm - the black man, the swamper, and the mentally disabled workhorse - collaborate in this dream. They are, metaphorically, the proletariat - the downtrodden workers of society - linking to form a socialist utopia. Or, at least, fantasizing about such a link. It's possible to go quite far with this socialist reading the more one knows about Marxist theory. One might look at Crooks' description of his past - when he had a farm of his own (81) - as a socialist "utopian past" from which the inequalities of capitalism have torn the worker. One might even consider George a kind of middle-class revolutionary leading the proletariat from their downtrodden position to a reunion with the natural cycles of labor. Of course, one ought to keep in mind that their revolution remains very small-scale - they desire merely to alter their own lives, not the lives of humanity at large - and nebulous. By the chapter's end, Crooks has utterly abandoned his dream of farm life.

It's also necessary to note that this fantasy farm does not seem to include women. Indeed, Curley's wife emerges in this chapter as both more complex and more loathsome than before. She is, on the one hand, much more than a one-dimensional harlot; at the same time, though, she represents a clear interruption of the socialist fantasy that the three men entertain. Indeed, she literally interrupts them at the height of their fantasizing. She is the snake - or, more to the point, the Eve - in the garden, the fact of life that makes a peaceful farm life so difficult, if not impossible, to obtain.

At the same time, at least she knows herself. We are allowed a glimpse into Curley's wife's discontent, and her frustration with life in some ways mirrors that of the three enfeebled men who have been left behind. She is especially comparable to Crooks; both are obviously intelligent and perceptive of themselves as well as others, and both contain a deep bitterness stemming from their mistreatment. The one is mistreated because he is black, the other because she is a woman. Both have a bleak and accurate insight into the fundamental nastiness of people. Curley's wife understands the deep-laden competitive urge for possessing women which tears men apart, and she knows that she is cast as the villain in this eternal game of one-upmanship.

However, she is also quick to act the villainous part. She knows how to use the unfairness of life to her advantage, which becomes disturbingly clear when she dangles the threat of crying rape in front of Crooks. She knows that as a black man he would be lynched if she told the others that he'd even tried to rape her, and she wields this power to her advantage. Ultimately, though, she is revealed as frightened of her husband as she sneaks off to her house. Curley's wife has been trapped by life, and however brazen and manipulative she may be, she is ultimately one of the comparatively powerless figures in the novel. She is therefore, perhaps, an object of the reader's sympathy.

As we near the climax of the novel, note how carefully Steinbeck has continued to develop the most conflict-laden thematic threads in the action. Curley's wife - the source of so much tension on the farm - and Lennie - who is capable of unthinking and brutal (if innocent) violence - have finally come into contact. Again, their relationship is subtly sexual. Curley's wife flirtatiously refers to Lennie as "Machine" (88) - revealing that she knows how her husband's hand was crushed and hinting that she "likes machines." Lennie is utterly incapable of dealing with this sort of flirtation. He is presented as a mere animal, drawn to Curley's wife by dumb instinct. Her effect on the horses as she exits clearly resonates with her effect on Lennie: "[W]hile she went through the barn, the halter chains rattled, and some horses snorted and some stamped their feet" (90). Lennie, who is both gentle and terribly dangerous, is at her mercy - which means, ultimately, that she is at his, though she doesn't know it yet.

Summary and Analysis of Chapter Five

Summary

The scene shifts to Sunday afternoon as Lennie sits in the barn, contemplating a dead puppy. He has killed his pup by petting it too hard. Lennie is gripped by a growing panic that George will find the dead puppy and that now he "won't get to tend the rabbits" (93).

Curley's wife enters in a dress decorated with red ostrich feathers. Lennie, who has been warned to have nothing to do with her, briefly tries to resist being drawn into conversation, but she prevails, telling him that the other men are too busy with their horseshoe tournament to care whether he talks to her or not. She sees the dead puppy and consoles him, saying that no one will care about the loss of a mere mutt.

She is clearly starved for conversation and launches into a reprise of her discontented story of what might have been. She insists that she could have been an actress. Lennie fails to understand her at all, however, as he continues to return to the dilemma of the dead puppy and his anxiety over being denied the right to tend the rabbits. Curley's wife angrily asks him why he is so obsessed with rabbits, and Lennie thoughtfully replies that he likes to pet nice things.

Curley's wife observes that Lennie is "[j]us' like a big baby" (99) and invites him to stroke her soft hair. Lennie begins to feel her hair and likes it very much indeed, which leads him to pet it too hard. Curley's wife begins to struggle, which sends Lennie into a panic. He grabs a hold of her hair and muffles her screams. When she continues to struggle, Lennie grows angry. He shakes her violently, telling her to keep quiet so that George doesn't hear her. Before he knows it, he has broken her neck. She lies dead on the hay. Lennie observes that he has "done a bad thing" (100) and covers her body with hay. He then disappears from the barn with the dead puppy in hand.

Candy comes looking for Lennie in the barn and discovers the body of Curley's wife. He fetches George, who knows exactly what has happened when he sees the body. Candy warns that Curley will lynch Lennie if they don't let him get away. After a sombre exchange in which Candy and George acknowledge that their dream of a farm can't amount to reality anymore, George decides the best course of action. He tells Candy to spread the news of the death to the rest of the men and to pretend that he (George) was never present in the barn. When George leaves, Candy scolds the corpse for being a "God damn tramp" (104).

Candy fetches the men and Curley immediately connects the killing to Lennie. He and Carlson run off to fetch guns. Meanwhile, George and Slim hypothesize that Lennie must have accidentally killed her, in the same way he got in trouble in Weed. George asks Slim whether Lennie might just be locked up and Slim replies that

Curley will want to shoot him. Carlson returns and announces that his Luger has been stolen. He blames Lennie for the theft.

Curley returns with a shotgun. He tells Whit to fetch the Soledad deputy sherrif, Al Whits, and organizes a posse from the rest of the men. George asks Curley not to shoot Lennie, but Curley refuses to listen, saying that Lennie is armed with the Luger. George deliberately misleads the posse, saying that Lennie would have headed south (rather than north, the direction from which they approached the farm). Curley warns George to join the hunt for Lennie "so we don't think you had nothin' to do with this" (108).

Analysis

This chapter contains what might be analyzed as the climactic action of the novel - the event after which there is no turning back. Once again, as in the previous chapters, the action centers around a single location - very much like a stage play. It's quite a fitting structure for the death of a would-be actress.

After he finds the body of Curley's wife, George notes that though Lennie does many "bad things," he never acts out of "meanness," only out of an inability to understand the world or control himself. George's choice of words is apt. Not only does "meanness" suggest "cruelty" - as in the childhood use of the word in the common phrase, "You're mean." "Meanness" also suggests small-mindedness or pettiness. Many of the characters in the novel act out of self-interested malice. Lennie never does. He acts with the best intentions at almost every turn; indeed (and despite his name) he has a simplicity of soul that contrasts starkly with the "smallness" of others. The word also suggests another variation - "meaning." Lennie doesn't mean to do bad things - they simply happen to him. He acts badly without intending to act at all.

Indeed, Lennie's crime is a fundamental inability to understand the frailty of others. He literally loves things to death. His puppy is soft, so he pets it to death. Only George understands him fully, knows his childish mixture of innocence and dangerousness. Others, including Curley's wife, treat him as a sort of sounding board for their own complaints and fantasies. Their failure to understand the danger that goes along with Lennie's obvious innocence results in the "bad things" that Lennie does. Crooks is just barely able to defuse Lennie's capacity for violent rage in the preceding chapter. Curley's wife, in this chapter, is not so lucky.

But then, the events of the chapter ought to surprise no one, really. They certainly don't surprise George or Slim, who are instantly able to determine from a look at Curley's wife that Lennie is the culprit and that he acted out of confused panic, just as he did at Weed. Lennie, like an animal, doesn't understand his actions as morally wrong. Rather, he thinks of them simply in terms of George's approval. Like a dog who feels a mixture of fear and love for his master, Lennie is both fiercely loyal to George and terrified of upsetting his friend. He knows instinctively that he has done something wrong both in killing the puppy and in killing Curley's wife. For Lennie, however, the two actions are roughly equivalent - in both cases, he simply feels that he risks losing George's permission to tend the rabbits. The question of the intrinsic value of human life never enters his thinking.

Curley's wife, as Steinbeck depicts her, does not share Lennie's innocence. Steinbeck rests a measure of blame for the killing on the victim herself. Again and again, Lennie's intrusion in the affairs of Curley and Curley's wife have been tinged with sex, and her offer to let Lennie touch her hair may be construed as a sexual advance. She even prefaces the offer by complaining of loneliness and dissatisfaction in her marriage. However sincere and pitiable these complaints may be, she is ultimately a self-absorbed, manipulative figure in the scene. She fails to understand the danger of Lennie - despite the evidence of his violent power in her husband's mutilated hand - and instead interprets his conflict with her husband and his fear of encountering her through a prism of vanity. She assumes that Lennie is her husband's babyish rival - a harmless admirer. Thus she "leads him on," to use the age-old misogynistic excuse for rape.

The full extent of the misogyny latent in the portrayal of Curley's wife comes following her death. Steinbeck describes her as having more life and vitality as a dead than a living character. The trope of finding beauty in a young woman's corpse is a very old one in Western literature - it can be found in countless texts, such as the dead Ophelia in *Hamlet*, or the dead maidens of Edgar Allen Poe's lyric poems. The basic idea in Steinbeck's description of Curley's wife's corpse is that in death her beauty can finally be appreciated apart from her conniving, duplicitous personality. It is as though he casts her sentience itself as her worst characteristic. In this way, she is completely objectified - reduced, in death, to the grotesque ideal of the silent and docile woman she never was in life. A modern reader has every reason to find this depiction objectionable.

Indeed, to pile indignity upon indignity, the final time we encounter her corpse occurs when Candy curses at it, calling her a tramp and a tart. Even in death she is nothing more than a scapegoat; and even her own husband fails to mourn her. Perhaps unintentionally, Steinbeck thus illustrates perfectly the horrible atmosphere of neglect and abuse that perhaps led her to act out in the first place. She was never considered as a person, only as Curley's problematic trophy.

We have seen so many threads of the story come together already, and the final plot movement of the story has a similarly inevitable trajectory. Steinbeck invites the reader to recall several additional associations in order to piece together the tragic resolution to come. We recall George's order from the beginning of the book - that if any trouble goes down, Lennie is to hide in the bushes near their original campsite. Thus we know that George has deliberately misled the posse by claiming that Lennie is likely headed south. Moreover, Carlton's missing Luger is highly significant. That was, after all, the gun that was used to shoot Candy's old sheep dog. The men assume that Lennie has stolen the weapon for his own protection - again revealing how little they understand Lennie, who is absolutely incapable of such calculation. The reader knows better, however.

Summary and Analysis of Chapter Six

Summary

The final chapter opens as Lennie waits in the bushes near the Salinas River, just as George told him to do in Chapter One. He nervously talks to himself, airing his worry that George won't let him tend the rabbits because of the bad things he did back at the ranch.

Lennie then hallucinates. He imagines the figure of his Aunt Clara - a plump, aproned woman with thick glasses - who scolds him for getting George into so much trouble. Lennie cries, begging Aunt Clara for forgiveness, and says that he will go off in the hills, where he can't bother George. Lennie then imagines a gigantic rabbit that mocks him for ever believing that he could tend the rabbits. The imaginary rabbit says that George will beat him with a stick when he arrives.

As Lennie sobs, George emerges from the brush. Lennie admits that he did a bad thing, but George appears not to care. Still upset, Lennie goads George into participating in their ritual routine of chastisement and forgiveness - he feeds George his lines about how much fun he would have if he didn't have to look after Lennie, and Lennie offers to go live in the hills and leave George alone. Lennie then requests the coup-de-grace: the story of how they're different from other workers and of how they'll have a farm together. George repeats these monologues woodenly.

He then tells Lennie to take off his hat as he continues to recount "how it will be" for them. He orders Lennie to kneel and pulls out Carlson's Luger. As the voices of the other men in the search party near their location, George tells Lennie one more time "about the rabbits," tells Lennie that they're going to get the farm right away, and shoots his companion in the back of the head.

Slim, Curley and Carlson arrive immediately after the shot is fired. Slim immediately interprets the scene accurately. Carlton and Curley, however, assume that George wrestled the Luger away from Lennie before shooting him. George, speaking in a whisper, affirms their false version of the events. The novel closes as Slim reassures George that he "had to do it," while Carlson and Curley look on in confusion, wondering why they are so upset.

Analysis

Steinbeck's careful control of setting in the novel is especially clear in this chapter, which finds us back at the beginning - at the brush near the Salinas River. As he did in the opening chapter, Steinbeck begins with a description of nature. Once again, this nature vignette resonates with the themes of the novel. We see the casual violence of nature - the stork devouring the water snake - and we see Lennie's nonchalant integration into this atmosphere as he stoops and drinks with his lips like a thirsty dog.

The content of Lennie's thoughts, and of Lennie and George's eventual conversation, also mirrors the opening. Lennie repeats the child-like, ritualistic cycle of separation and reconciliation that has seemingly marked his relationship with George for years. Once again he hears George complain that he could live it up if not for Lennie; once again he offers to leave George and live in the hills; once again he gets George to tell him about their rabbit utopia.

However, these similarities - the setting and the content - only ultimately emphasize how much has changed since the novel's opening. Where George was once full of life - angry and forgiving - now he is a husk of himself, bereft of emotion as he goes through his monologues. What was once a plausible - if far-fetched - fantasy has disintegrated into delusion. He knows what must happen, even as Lennie goes on believing in the rabbits. Whereas in Chapter One we see George and Lennie's "best laid plans," here in Chapter Six we have irrefutable evidence that, just as Robert Burns' poem predicts, these plans have gone awry.

Emphasizing the delusional nature of Lennie's point-of-view, Steinbeck adapts his one experimental narrative gesture in the novel, choosing to depict two hallucinations - first Aunt Clara, and then (more ludicrous still) a giant sardonic rabbit. It is unclear whether we are supposed to understand these hallucinations to be one-time phenomena or regularly recurring. (By the way, the reader may find it a bit unbelievable that this gentle giant, who everywhere else proves incapable of understanding figurative language, is able to imaginatively generate such colorful self-chastisements as "you ain't worth a greased jack-pin to ram you into hell" (112).)

Either way, Chapter Six represents our closest approach to Lennie's experience - his simultaneous fear and love of authority figures, his relentless obsession with the rabbits, and his constant (if confused) regret that he never fails to act in a confused and problematic way. Lennie, social pack animal that he is, has a deep-seated need for discipline and forgiveness. His self-chastisement is quite moving, both because it reveals a degree of self-understanding in Lennie and because it suggests that he is regularly and brutally upset with himself. His remorse hardly counts as a conscience - at no point does he register that he has committed murder, only that he has done yet another inscrutable "bad thing" - but it makes a claim on the reader's sympathy nevertheless.

George's mercy killing of Lennie neatly parallels the events of Chapter Three, when Candy allowed Carlson to shoot his malodorous old dog. Steinbeck is even careful to involve the same Luger in each killing. Whereas the meek and passive Candy proved unable to do the job himself, George shows no such weakness. As has been proven beyond a reasonable doubt at this point, Lennie's lethal innocence is not compatible with the world. He cannot learn to change his ways - he cannot even understand why the "bad things" he has done are bad. The fate he would meet at Curley's (mutilated) hands - likely a drawn-out, vengeful lynching - is enough to convince George that his only real option is to make Lennie's death as quick and painless as possible.

At the novel's end, a few haunting questions remain. Why, after all, is George so attached to Lennie? What did he gain from the infantile and troublesome giant's companionship? Many theories have emerged over the years, as readers and critics have speculated that George is somehow specifically in Aunt Clara's debt, that George and Lennie are actually related after all, or even that George and Lennie are in love - romantically, not merely as friends. However, before (or at least alongside) such speculation, it's important to note that Steinbeck deliberately chooses to leave this central question murky. In a novel so carefully wrought in all other respects, this central motivational ambiguity stands as a deliberate and unsolvable mystery.

The simple answer may be that in the callous world of the itinerant laborer, the constant loyalty and companionship of a man like Lennie acts as an antidote to alienation. Lennie, paradoxically, represents the instinctual innocence in life. Writers as diverse as William Blake in his *Songs of Innocence* or Mark Twain in *The Mysterious Stranger* have explored the interesting ways in which innocence is not, in fact, altogether innocent. Divorced from a sense of good and evil, the truly innocent are capable of performing acts of apparent cruelty without remorse. Lennie is just such an innocent. He tempers George's worldly weariness with the constant presence of discovery and hope even as he plagues George's life with the threat of misunderstanding and ignorant folly. In many ways, Lennie completes George. And as his hollow despair at the close of the novel suggests, George ultimately needs Lennie's innocence just as much as Lennie depends on George's experience.

Suggested Essay Questions

1. How does the setting of *Of Mice and Men* influence the book's thematic development? In answering, consider the connection between the novel's setting and the characters' vocations. Also, how does Steinbeck signal the importance of setting in his choice of place names?

   Though the novel is more famous for its characters than its setting, *Of Mice and Men* could not have been set elsewhere than in the rural Salinas valley of California. The problems of the novel are intimately tied to the rhythms and frustrations of the itinerant worker's life. Shifting from ranch to ranch, from one menial job to another, the Californian itinerant worker risked a life of meaningless labor - of pure, cynical sustenance. George and Lennie, with their dream of acquiring a farm, represent an attempt to stand against such perpetual loneliness. Even the name of the city near which the novel is set - Soledad, which is Spanish for "solitude" - resonates with this theme of loneliness.
2. The title, *Of Mice and Men*, is an allusion to a Robert Burns poem. How is this allusion meaningful in the novel? Consider some similarities and differences between Burns and Steinbeck's works.

   Robert Burns' poem, "To a Mouse," is the source of the famous quotation: "The best laid schemes o' Mice an' Men / Gang aft agley" ("often go awry"). And, indeed, *Of Mice and Men* features two men with a scheme - to escape their lives of menial, temporary employment - that goes awry. Beyond this simple plot similarity, the two works both consider the relationship between the human and animal worlds. Burns poem, in which a field worker offers philosophical reflections after upsetting a mouse's nest, mirrors Steinbeck's work, in which Lennie unintentionally destroys the lives of small, furry animals (including, at the novel's opening, a mouse, which is a clear wink at the Burns poem).
3. *Of Mice and Men* is highly "dramatic" - that is, similar to a drama or play - in its structure and action. Describe the ways in which the novel is like a play. Why did Steinbeck choose to put his work together in this way?

   Each chapter of the novel takes place in a single location, aside from a short walk at the beginning of Chapter One. Thus the novel is structured, much like a play, into "scenes." The locations of these scenes are treated much like the space of a stage - characters enter and exit frequently, give speeches and move the plot forward. The narrator, meanwhile, is minimally intrusive. This "dramatic" form of writing allows the novel to progress rapidly and portentously, building symbolic density and narrative tension without becoming too heavy-handed. It also, by the way, allowed *Of Mice and Men* to be adapted for the stage almost immediately after its publication.
4. *Of Mice and Men* is often studied as an example of "foreshadowing" in

literature. How does Steinbeck foreshadow the pivotal events of the book? What does this effect do for the tone of the book?

Nearly every word and image in the novel is carefully chosen to guide the reader to the accidental killing of Curley's wife and the mercy killing of Lennie. The gun used to shoot Candy's decrepit dog is later used by George to shoot Lennie; the many small animals that Lennie crushes out of love foreshadow his panicked killings of his puppy and, moments later, Curley's wife; and the event that drove George and Lennie out of Weed (Lennie's false accusation of rape) parallels the scene in the barn between him and Curley's wife. This dense layering of related plot elements gives the plot an element of inevitability - as though fate has preordained the tragic events of the book.

5. Several of the characters in *Of Mice and Men* display physical and mental impairments. Identify and describe these characters. How do these impairments influence or reflect these characters' roles in the novel?

   Of Mice and Men is a novel about impairments, both literal and symbolic. Most of the men in the novel are impaired in some fundamental way, most often in terms of their loneliness and isolation. In the case of several characters, this symbolic impairment becomes expressed literally through their damaged bodies. Crooks and Candy are hunch-backed and lame; Curley's hand is crushed (an injury which reflects on his damaged masculinity in general). The most conspicuously impaired person in the novel, Lennie, is impaired in an altogether different way. Bodily, he is the most able man in the novel, but mentally, he is incompatible with social life. Thus the different nature of his disability reflects and emphasizes his inability to survive in the lonely, desolate environment of the itinerant worker.

6. Consider Curley's wife. Is she a sympathetic or an unsympathetic character? Would you characterize Steinbeck's portrayal of her as fair, or do you detect misogyny in his depiction?

   Curley's wife, the only major character who is not given an individual name, is indeed an enigma. In the first chapters of the book, she is simply awful - a flirtatious, provocative "tramp," to use Candy's word for her. However, in the later part of the book we do get a glimpse at a richer inner-life as she speaks about her loneliness, her regrets, and her unhappy marriage. On the whole, however, Steinbeck's depiction of Curley's wife is quite disturbing from the perspective of a modern reader.

7. Discuss "the rabbits," the dream of a farm that George and Lennie share and repeat aloud. How does this story of "how things will be" function in the novel? What does it reveal about George, Lennie, and their relationship?

   The story of "how things will be" comes off much like a bedtime story - an oft-repeated tale (which Lennie even has memorized, much like a child memorizes his favorite stories) that has a soothing, dream-like effect on both teller and listener. The parental nature of George and Lennie's relationship is quite clear in these passages, as George (the parent) uses the story to soothe and encourage Lennie (the child). This ritualistic recitation provides their work with meaning and purpose; by the end of the novel, though, as the tragic current of the book proves irresistible, the story takes on a poignant quality.

8. *Of Mice and Men* opens and closes in a natural setting. The chapters in between take place in various man-made settings - the bunk house, the barn, Crooks' room. Why does Steinbeck organize the novel in this way? In general, what does he propose about the relationship between man and nature?

   In opening and closing his novel in nature, Steinbeck is able to connect and compare the actions of his characters with the natural world. The nature scenes comment on the events in question - George and Lennie disrupt a peaceful scene in the opening; the killing of a snake by a heron prefigures the tragedy in the final chapter. Not only does this way of structuring the novel give it a feeling of wholeness, it also reinforces Steinbeck's central point about Lennie's incompatibility with the social world. He doesn't fit in the shared spaces - the bunk house, etc. - while, in contrast, he romanticizes the natural world, repeatedly promising to live "like a bear" in a cave. Of course, Lennie is not a bear, however similar he may be to one. He can't life with men, and he can't live without them; therefore, in the end, he can't live at all.

9. Consider the scene in Crooks' room. How does Steinbeck characterize Crooks and the others, and how does the conversation in the chapter play out in the context of the novel as a whole?

   Crooks is a proud, embittered man - a victim of racism. The scene that takes place in his room illustrates several tendencies in the novel. For one thing, Lennie is able to win Crooks over despite (or, actually, by virtue of) his opacity; this allows the reader to see Lennie's appeal as a nonjudgmental, faithful companion. Also, when Crooks rouses Lennie's anger, we see more evidence of the dangerous rage that lurks beneath Lennie's placid exterior. Finally, the appearance of Candy allows Steinbeck to stage a sort of socialist fantasy, in which the downtrodden, disabled members of the farm contemplate a mild "uprising" of sorts. The appearance of Curley's wife, though, returns these men to the direness of their social situation. Thus the chapter functions almost as a microcosm for the novel as a whole, as we move from hope to hopelessness, with Curley's wife as a catalyst for trouble.

10. *Of Mice and Men* has a controversial history. It has been repeatedly banned by school boards. Why might this book have been banned? Is such an action justified?

There are several reasons for the novel's controversial reputation. Most obviously, the novel features frank discussion of sexual matters - rape, prostitution, promiscuity - that has been targeted as possibly inappropriate for a young audience. Also, the novel ends in a morally ambiguous killing - similar to euthanasia - which has roused the ire of several anti-euthanasia advocacy groups. Though it is well-established as required reading in thousands of high school districts throughout the world, the book continues to attract controversy. The question of whether or not the book is offensive is of course a matter of personal morals; however, Steinbeck's treatment of such sensitive material has been generally celebrated for its tastefulness and honesty.

The Mentally Impaired in Classic Literature

English teaching at the Middle and High School levels shows a perhaps surprising propensity for literature that features the intellectually and/or developmentally impaired. *Of Mice and Men* is only one such novel. Ken Kesey's *One Flew Over the Cuckoo's Nest*, which is often assigned in high school English classes, is narrated by an American Indian man who is feigning near-catatonic stupidity. Similarly, Carson McCuller's classic novel, *The Heart Is a Lonely Hunter*, features a deaf-mute who is also described as imbecilic. Boo Radley, the mysterious shut-in in Harper Lee's *To Kill a Mockingbird*, is also a centrally important figure. And the widely taught short story (and subsequent novel) *Flowers for Algernon* by Daniel Keyes features a mentally retarded man who, due to miraculous medical treatment, is temporarily enhanced to a genius-level intellect. Several other classic novels that are less widely taught in schools, including Fyodor Dostoevsky's *The Idiot*, Graham Greene's *A Burnt-Out Case*, and William Faulkner's *The Sound and the Fury*, also feature mentally and physically challenged characters in central roles.

The question of why such a broad array of novels featuring the mentally impaired have proved so popular in the English curriculum is difficult to address briefly, but a few patterns seem clear. These novels are almost always quite sombre and pessimistic - exploring issues of social isolation, alienation and crisis - and these highly teachable, symbolically rich issues inevitably hinge on the mentally impaired individual in the novel. These characters serve as allegorical representations of a universal impairment that, the authors often suggest, is part of the human condition in general.

In *Of Mice and Men*, Lennie's extreme unsuitability for the social world provides Steinbeck with a means for exploring the needs and weaknesses of all his characters. For instance, Lennie is a foil for Curley's wife's confessions of unhappiness; he is a means for Candy's dream of replacing his dog with a new companionship; he tempers George's natural cynicism, giving his friend a sense of meaning and ambition for the future. In short, Lennie's extreme dependence on others represents every character's need for companionship. He is the symbol of alienation in general.

Similarly, in the other novels mentioned above, the central "idiot" figures provide a quick and concrete means of reflecting on the alienating cruelty of society in general. These characters are thus, almost inevitably, allegorical mutations of "man-in-general." Because the High School and College English curriculum so often prioritizes literature that highlights symbolism and universal-philosophical ponderings, it's quite easy to see why these novels, with their central symbol-characters, have proved so popular.

In recent years, a field in English Studies has emerged to challenge this treatment of the disabled as allegory: variously termed Disability or Dis/ability Studies. Scholars in this field often write about mentally and physically disabled characters as "marginalized individuals" - in other words, as human beings who have been systematically misunderstood and mistreated - rather than symbols of "man's isolation" or some other universal, allegorical interpretation.

Scholars in Disability Studies vary in their work, obviously, but many emphasize that the prevalent reading of the mentally and physically challenged as "universal symbols" is not necessarily inherent to the novels so much as it is to the *teaching* of the novels. For instance, one could easily read *Of Mice and Men* as a study of a "marginalized individual" rather than one of universal isolation as captured in Lennie. In general, such an approach encourages a consideration of the factors that lead a character like Lennie to end up in a situation of such ill fit. In other words, they replace the question that is so often asked of Lennie - why or why not is he unfit for society? - with a new question - what are the parameters of "social fitness" in the novel and how are they upheld?

Author of ClassicNote and Sources

W.C. Miller, author of ClassicNote. Completed on July 30, 2008, copyright held by GradeSaver.

Updated and revised Damien Chazelle November 30, 2008. Copyright held by GradeSaver.

Jackson J. Benson. The Short Novels of John Steinbeck. Durham, N.C.: Duke University Press, 1990.

Harold Bloom. Of Mice and Men: Bloom's Notes. New York: Chelsea House, 1996.

Charlotte Hadella. Of Mice and Men: A Kinship of Powerlessness. Upper Saddle River, N.J.: Prentice Hall, 1995.

John Steinbeck. Of Mice and Men. New York: Bantam Books, 1965.

Susan Shillinglaw. "John Steinbeck, American Writer." 2008-08-21. <http://www.steinbeck.sjsu.edu/biography/briefbiography.jsp>.

Essay: Violence and Sadism in John Steinbeck's Of Mice and Men

by Anonymous
April 10, 2003

In John Steinbeck's powerful American masterpiece Of Mice and Men, first published in 1937 during the height of the Great Depression, the main characters of George Milton and Lennie Small experience many hard and difficult situations which on occasion are steeped with violence and sadistic behavior, due to living and working in "a world where personal interaction is marked by. . . petty control, misunderstanding, jealousy and callousness" (Scheer 14). Yet after a careful reading of the text, it becomes clear that George and Lennie are at times the true instigators of the violence while also being pawns in the hands of such men as Curley, the prizefighter who finds much sadistic delight in picking on the ranch workers and those whom he sees as socially beneath him.

Interestingly, Steinbeck himself was quite familiar with the trials and tribulations associated with being an outsider and a common laborer, much like George and Lennie in Of Mice and Men. During his youth, Steinbeck worked diligently as a hired hand on ranches close to his home in Salinas, California, where he met and talked with migrant farm workers who told him of their adventures and mishaps before and during the Great Depression when millions of people were unemployed and were forced to earn their living by any means necessary. These chance meetings and descriptions of what it was like to be a common laborer served Steinbeck well, for he later incorporated many of these down-and-out tales into his novels and short stories, Of Mice and Men being no exception.

If we examine some of the major scenes in Of Mice and Men, the presence of

violence and sadism can easily be sensed, especially through the actions and reactions of Lennie Small, the lumbering giant with the mind of a child who brings a frightening capacity for violence into the unsuspecting bunkhouse at the ranch. As William Goldhurst points out, Lennie "carries with him, intact from childhood, that low threshold between rage and pleasure which we all carry within us into adulthood" (135), yet in the hands of those most prone to sadistic behavior, Lennie is a scapegoat and thus cannot be held accountable for his actions, due to his mental capacity which borders on imbecility.

In the scene where George and Lennie are on their way to the ranch to buck barley, the conversation turns to their last job in the little town of Weed, where Lennie had been attracted to a girl's red dress. After grabbing at her clothes, Lennie became so frightened by her screaming that George was forced to hit him over to head to make him let go of her. Following this incident, the duo ends up being chased by a mob out to lynch them for Lennie's treatment of the girl which in the eyes of the lynch mob was akin to attempted rape. In essence, this scene illustrates Steinbeck's power as a writer with his ability to bring into extraordinary scenes of social conflict the psychological forcefulness of Lennie's infantile reactions to the girl's red dress. But the violence of Lennie towards the girl pales in comparison to the violent reactions of the mob who are obviously either unaware of Lennie's child-like mind or simply see the situation as an opportunity to express their inner anger towards "a subhuman creature, unable to distinguish between right and wrong" (Benson 256).

The initial introduction of Curley, the swaggering, boastful son of the ranch owner, truly sets the stage for more violence and sadistic behavior aimed at not only George and Lennie but anyone who stands in his way or throws a glancing eye towards his attractive yet whorish wife. During the time when George and Lennie are waiting for the lunch bell, Curley enters the bunkhouse, ostensibly looking for his father but really just to examine the new hired men. After putting across to the men that he is the master of the ranch, Curley leaves and Candy, the swamper who sweeps out the bunkhouse, warns George and Lennie about Curley's temper and his eagerness to fight anyone who usurps his authority. But in this instance, George could be viewed as the instigator to the violence that follows, for he calls Curley's wife "a rat-trap, a bitch, and a piece of jail-bait" (Goldhurst 130), and later fully expresses his disgust at Curley's glove full of vaseline, aimed at softening his hand when he stroke's his wife's genitalia. But again, Curley could have simply laughed at George and shrugged it off instead of using this episode as a springboard for more violence and sadism. Incidentally, when the other men in the bunkhouse taunt Curley about his wife's wantonness and he spies Lennie grinning about it, Curley attacks Lennie who at first does nothing to defend himself because of George's warning about his strength. But then, due to his imbecility, Lennie grabs Curley's hand, the one with the vaseline glove, and squeezes it, thereby crushing every bone.

But the most important scene in Of Mice and Men concerns the killing of Curley's wife in the barn by Lennie. As the other workmen and George are pitching horseshoes outside the barn, Lennie suddenly realizes that his puppy, given to him by Slim, the jerkline skinner, is dead as a result of his seemingly gentle and innocent caresses. As he sits down in the straw and bemoans the puppy's fate, Curley's wife quickly appears from around the corner of the stalls. Her flirtatious behavior at first does not affect Lennie and he doesn't say one word to her, fearing that he would not get to feed the rabbits which George promised to him upon obtaining their own ranch. But Curley's wife gradually manages to draw Lennie's attention away from the dead puppy and initiates a rather curious incident--she convinces him to stroke her hair which he does as if she was just another plaything like his dead puppy.

As Lennie continues to stroke the girl's hair, she suddenly tries to pull

away which infuriates Lennie, especially when she starts to scream. And just like the puppy, Lennie becomes a little to rough and breaks her neck without any awareness that she provoked her own death, due to not knowing that Lennie is nothing but a lumbering idiot with the strength of a plow horse.

According to Jackson J. Benson, this scene from Of Mice and Men contains images of great power and violence, for it makes "murder seem as natural and innocent as puppy love" (179). As a very sizable child, Lennie amplifies the entire situation, for after killing Curley's wife, he flees to the grove near the Salinas River just as George had told him in case of any "accidents" on Lennie's part. But this time around, George appears to be the sadist, for Lennie begins to think about living in a cave if George decides he doesn't want him around anymore.

The final scene in Of Mice and Men brings the plot full circle, for Lennie's contradictory values are then affirmed--his blameless, animal instincts mixed with sad humanity, his innocent longings for a pen full of rabbits which he can pet and tend to, and his grim awareness that his life may be nearing its end. When Candy, the bunkhouse sweeper, finds Curley's wife half-buried and stone dead in the hay in the barn, he calls for George who gets a gun while Candy spreads the alarm that the girl has been murdered. But when Curely is told of his wife's death, his sadistic tendencies come to a boil, for he realizes that Lennie is to blame which sets into motion a true cycle of vengeance on the part of Curley and the other hired hands at the ranch. With a loaded shotgun in hand, Curley and the other men start out in search of Lennie, the poor, dumb brute with a tendency for childish violence.

But it is George who finds Lennie hiding in the bushes near the Salinas River, and soon makes up his mind to put an end to Lennie's life, to punish him once more for "being a bad boy." But for Lennie, badness is just a matter of opinion and taboos based on the mind of an imbecile, not consequences and responsibilities, for he does not care about nor understand the death of Curley's wife who exists for him only as another lifeless puppy or a mouse dead from too much hard handling.

In the conclusion of Steinbeck's Of Mice and Men, George puts the muzzle of his gun to the back of Lennie's head and pulls the trigger, an action which fully supports and reinforces the violence in the novel. In essence, all of the characters in Of Mice and Men seem to have been reared in violence; some are violent by nature, while others simply accept violent, sadistic behavior as part of the "normal" life of a drifter or a migrant farm worker. As Frank N. Magill so acutely observes, "both George and Lennie are friendless and alone and prone to destructive violence. Both are adolescents caught in a world of chaos and rage" (2145), exactly as John Steinbeck intended it. In his words, these characters exist in "sweet violence" which moves the reader to contemplate their puzzling fates.

BIBLIOGRAPHY

Benson, Jackson J. The True Adventures of John Steinbeck, Writer. New York: Viking Press, 1984.

Goldhurst, William. "Of Mice & Men: John Steinbeck's Parable of the Curse of Cain." Western American Literature. 6 (Summer 1971): 123-35.

Magill, Frank N., ed. Masterplots: Digests of World Literature. New York: Salem Press, 1964.

Scheer, Ronald. "Of Mice & Men: Novel, Play, Movie." The American Examiner. Vol. VI (Fall/Winter 1978-79): 6-39.

Essay: Camaraderie: Deciding an Individual's Fate

by Sarma Vemuri
July 09, 2005

Of Mice and Men and The Grapes of Wrath, two novels published concurrently by John Steinbeck, both depict camaraderie between dust bowl migrants. The main characters in Of Mice and Men, George and Lennie, form a bond, while struggling to reach their goal, a small farm. Similarly, Jim Casy of The Grapes of Wrath befriends Tom Joad, a friendship eventually uplifting the whole migrant community. Outwardly, the two relationships may seem to parallel each other. In reality, these alliances differ greatly. Consequently, in Of Mice and Men, friendship leads to destruction, in The Grapes of Wrath, salvation. Starkly contrasting George and Lennie's relationship in Of Mice and Men to Tom and Jim Casy's in The Grapes of Wrath, Steinbeck unquestionably shows that camaraderie decides an individual's fate.

To begin, George and Lennie interact quite differently from Tom and Casy; the former share a master-slave relationship, while the latter, a more equal relationship. For instance, George orders Lennie to ìsay nothingî(6), upon reaching the ranch where they will work, fearing that if "[the boss] finds out what a crazy bastard [Lennie is], [they] won't get no job" (6). Lennie obeys. Later on, when Lennie innocently calls Curley's wife, the flirtatious daughter-in-law of the ranch owner, "purty" (32), George fiercely admonishes Lennie to not "even look at that bitch" (32), once again demonstrating a master-slave relationship. In contrast, Tom and Casy, engage in an equal relationship; in fact, Tom candidly tells Casy, a one-time preacher, now philosopher, his opinion of Casy's philosophy, throughout The Grapes of Wrath. For example, when Casy explains to Tom his idea that "maybe all men got one big soul ever'body's a part of"(33), Tom openly replies, "you can't hold no church with idears like that" (33). Moreover, Casy never forces Tom to do anything, contrasting their relationship to George and Lennie's relationship. Actually, at the conclusion of The Grapes of Wrath, Casy only requests Tom to "- tell the folks [in the ranch] how it is - Tell 'em their starvin' [the protesters] an' stabbin' theirself in the back" (523); Tom replies "I'll try to get to tell the folks" (523). Clearly, Tom and Casy's equal relationship sets them apart from George and Lennie's master-slave interaction. These relationships, in turn, decide the fate of the respective characters.

Not only do the relationships contrast each other, they also shape the people involved differently. In The Grapes of Wrath, Tom Joad transforms from self-centered person to a martyr for all "Okie" (280) people, because of his companionship with Casy. Initially, a very hedonistic Tom remarks, "Maybe I should of been a preacher - I been a long time without a girl" (31). This self-indulgent outlook gives way to a broader, all-encompassing attitude, as Casy's philosophy influences him. Before leaving his family, in the concluding chapters of The Grapes of Wrath, Tom explains to his mother, "Maybe like Casy says, a fella ain't got a soul of his own, but a big piece of one" (572), he even adds "God, I'm talkin' like Casy - comes to thinkin' about him so much" (572). Obviously, Tom's camaraderie with Casy transforms Tom for the better; however, in Of Mice and Men, George virtually crushes Lennie's free will, making Lennie completely dependent upon him. For example, Lennie initially threatens to "go off in the hills an' find a cave" (12), whenever George treats him cruelly; thereby, Lennie exerts a measure of freedom. However, as the story progresses, Lennie seems to have no will of his own. In fact, when Curley, the ranch owner's belligerent son, fights with Lennie, George must command Lennie to "get 'im" (63); subsequently, when Lennie nearly kills Curley, George must order Lennie to "leggo of him" (63). Therefore, Lennie's transformation reflects his relationship with George, a master-slave partnership, transforming Lennie for the worse. Later on, in each novel, the deaths that occur reflect the wide gulf between the respective associations.

Finally, Casy and Lennie's deaths contrastingly impact each relationship; Lennie's death for the worse, Casy's death for the better. In Of Mice and Men, Lennie's unswerving devotion to George leads to his own death, when Curley's wife flirts with him. At first, Lennie scorns her advances saying "[if] George sees me talkin' to you, he'll give me hell" (87). Curley's wife persists, even letting Lennie stroke her hair. When Lennie pulls to hard on her hair, she beings to scream, scaring Lennie; Lennie believes that if George hears her screaming, George won't let him ìtend the rabbitsî(87), at their dream ranch. In a moment of confusion, Lennie accidentally kills Curley's wife; then, he goes to "hide in the brush till [George] comes" (92), carrying out George's instructions to the letter. Sadly, George, Lennie's so-called friend, shoots Lennie, when he comes to the brush. Lennie's death sharply contrasts Casy's death, which inspires Tom to champion the ìOkieî(280) cause. Throughout The Grapes of Wrath, Casy's philosophy affects Tom subtle ways. Casy's death acts as a catalyst, making Tom realize the truth behind Casy's theories. However, both deaths influence the respective relationships differently; Lennie's negatively, Casy's positively.

Thus, John Steinbeck deliberately contrasts George and Lennie's master-slave relationship to Tom and Casy's equal relationship, to show that camaraderie shapes a character's fate. Both Casy and George cause changes in Tom and Lennie, respectively. However, Tom changes from a hedonistic individual to a martyr for the "Okie"(280) peoples; contrastingly, George affects a negative change is Lennie. Lennie, who has some degree of free will initially, becomes completely dependent upon George. In both cases, the old adage, "Beware of the company you keep" holds true, for the company the characters keep eventually transforms them for the better or for the worse.

Quiz 1

1. **Why do George and Lennie leave the ranch in Weed?**
    A. Lennie fought with the farmer's son-in-law.
    B. Lennie and George were fired.
    C. Lennie was accused of rape.
    D. Lennie killed the farmer's rabbit.

2. **For what does Lennie ask that angers George?**
    A. A Puppy
    B. Rabbits
    C. Ketchup
    D. Beans

3. **According to George, why are he and Lennie different from other migrant laborers?**
    A. They have a chance to fulfill their dream of owning land.
    B. They are not lonely, for they have each other.
    C. They don't have any responsibilities.
    D. They cannot move from job to job as easily because of Lennie's disability.

4. **Which of the following does not foreshadow later events in the novel?**
    A. George scolds Lennie for getting them fired from every job they have.
    B. George talks about Aunt Clara.
    C. George kills the mouse that he holds.
    D. George tells Lennie where to hide if there is trouble.

5. **Which of the following does not describe Lennie?**
    A. Innocent
    B. Talkative
    C. Forgetful
    D. Slow-witted

6. **Which of the following is not significant about George's speech to Lennie?**
    A. The speech demonstrates Lennie's fixation in simplistic pleasures.
    B. George's dreams for the future contrast with their current situation.
    C. The speech foreshadows George and Lennie's future together.
    D. George has given the speech many times, showing the tenacity with which they hold their dreams.

7. **Which of the following is not a possible reason why the boss suspects George and Lennie?**
   A. Lennie does not speak.
   B. George gives an unsatisfactory answer why they are no longer in Weed.
   C. Lennie appears foolish and dimwitted.
   D. George shows concern for Lennie.

8. **Why does Curley dislike Lennie?**
   A. Curley is jealous of those who are bigger than he.
   B. Lennie ogles his wife.
   C. Lennie laughs at Curley.
   D. The boss tells Curley to watch out for Lennie.

9. **What is the significance of George's explanation that he and Lennie are cousins?**
   A. It explains why George cares for Lennie despite his apparent dislike for him.
   B. He lies because Lennie believes that he is George's actual cousin.
   C. This lie alerts the boss that George and Lennie are trouble.
   D. They are in an environment in which two men can only behave kindly to one another if they have a tangible family connection.

10. **What do the men think of Curley's Wife?**
    A. They suspect that she married Curley because she is pregnant.
    B. They think that she is a tart.
    C. They think that she married Curley for money.
    D. They pity her for her marriage to Curley.

11. **Which of the following does not describe Curley's Wife when she first enters the bunk house?**
    A. Worried
    B. Seductive
    C. Confrontational
    D. Angry

12. **Which of the following is not significant about George's story about the river?**
    A. It shows that Lennie will obey George unconditionally.
    B. It shows that George is capable of cruelty toward Lennie.
    C. It shows that Lennie is an innocent who does not know the consequences of his actions.
    D. It shows that Lennie is capable of self-inflicted violence.

13. **Which of the following is not an explanation for why Lennie and George travel together?**
    A. George fears becoming violent if left to himself.
    B. Lennie needs constant supervision.
    C. George feels responsible for Lennie.
    D. Lennie is George's only surviving relative.

14. **Which of the ranch workers has a dog that recently had a litter of puppies?**
    A. Crooks
    B. Carlson
    C. Slim
    D. Candy

15. **Which of these animals is not killed in the course of the story?**
    A. A mouse
    B. A puppy
    C. A rabbit
    D. An old dog

16. **Which of the following does not describe Candy?**
    A. passive
    B. malleable
    C. dependent
    D. ill-tempered

17. **Which of these comparisons between Candy and his dog does not hold true?**
    A. Candy and his dog are both outcasts.
    B. Candy and his dog are both aged and decrepit.
    C. Candy and his dog are both barely able to function without others' help.
    D. Candy and his dog are both sacrificed when useless.

18. **Why does Candy let Carlson shoot his dog?**
    A. Candy is pressured into letting Carlson shoot his dog.
    B. Candy cannot afford the dog anymore.
    C. Candy knows that his dog will only suffer if he lives.
    D. Carlson offers Candy another dog.

19. **Where does George go at night without Lennie?**
    A. a strip joint
    B. a pool hall
    C. to sleep with Curley's wife
    D. a whorehouse

20. **Which of the following characters does not remain at the farm at night?**
    A. Lennie
    B. Crooks
    C. Slim
    D. Candy

21. **What does Lennie do when Curley punches him?**
    A. He does not fight back.
    B. He immediately crushes Curley's hand.
    C. He attempts to strange Curley.
    D. He begins to weep.

22. **Which of the following is not a dangerous woman in the novel?**
    A. The 'tart'
    B. Aunt Clara
    C. The woman from Weed
    D. Curley's Wife

23. **What is the name of Curley's Wife?**
    A. Colleen
    B. Beatrice
    C. She is never named.
    D. Clara

24. **According to Crooks, what would happen to Lennie without George?**
    A. He would live like an animal.
    B. He would be sent to an insane asylum.
    C. He would be unable to support himself.
    D. He would end up killing himself.

25. **According to Curley's wife, under what condition do men speak to her?**

A. When she behaves like a proper wife.

B. When Curley is around.

C. When she offers sexual favors.

D. When they are alone.

Quiz 1 Answer Key

1. **(C)** Lennie was accused of rape.
2. **(C)** Ketchup
3. **(B)** They are not lonely, for they have each other.
4. **(B)** George talks about Aunt Clara.
5. **(B)** Talkative
6. **(C)** The speech foreshadows George and Lennie's future together.
7. **(C)** Lennie appears foolish and dimwitted.
8. **(A)** Curley is jealous of those who are bigger than he.
9. **(D)** They are in an environment in which two men can only behave kindly to one another if they have a tangible family connection.
10. **(B)** They think that she is a tart.
11. **(D)** Angry
12. **(D)** It shows that Lennie is capable of self-inflicted violence.
13. **(D)** Lennie is George's only surviving relative.
14. **(C)** Slim
15. **(C)** A rabbit
16. **(B)** malleable
17. **(A)** Candy and his dog are both outcasts.
18. **(A)** Candy is pressured into letting Carlson shoot his dog.
19. **(D)** a whorehouse
20. **(C)** Slim
21. **(A)** He does not fight back.
22. **(B)** Aunt Clara
23. **(C)** She is never named.
24. **(B)** He would be sent to an insane asylum.
25. **(D)** When they are alone.

Quiz 2

1. **Why does George prefer whores to other women?**
    A. He does not have to commit to a prostitute.
    B. He knows what a prostitute expects.
    C. He actually prefers decent women to whores.
    D. He likes the added risks of seeing prostitutes.

2. **What is the threat that Curley's wife makes in Crooks' cabin?**
    A. She threatens to have the men fired.
    B. She threatens to have Crooks lynched.
    C. She threatens to accuse Lennie of rape.
    D. She threatens to send Curley after them.

3. **What does Crooks say that upsets Lennie?**
    A. He says that Lennie might be insane.
    B. He says that Lennie and Candy are cripples.
    C. He says that Lennie and George will never own a farm.
    D. He says that George might leave Lennie.

4. **How does Lennie kill the puppy?**
    A. He smothers it.
    B. He allows the puppy to drown.
    C. He bounces the puppy too hard.
    D. He strangles the puppy.

5. **What is Lennie's reaction when he kills the puppy?**
    A. He becomes angry at the puppy.
    B. He immediately begs for forgiveness.
    C. He does not realize that the puppy is actually dead.
    D. He is unconcerned.

6. **Which of the following is the best explanation for the behavior of Curley's wife around Lennie?**
    A. She wanted to frame Lennie.
    B. She wanted companionship.
    C. She wanted to make Curley jealous.
    D. She wanted to seduce Lennie.

7. **What is Candy's reaction to the death of Curley's wife?**
   A. He believes that Lennie murdered Curley's wife out of anger.
   B. He worries that he will be fired for what has happened.
   C. He worries that this will upset their plans to get a place together.
   D. He blames George for leaving Lennie alone.

8. **Which of the following does Lennie not do when he escapes the farm?**
   A. He follows George's orders and hides by the river.
   B. He finds a rabbit.
   C. He hallucinates that he sees Aunt Clara.
   D. He talks to himself.

9. **What is Carlson's reaction to Lennie's death?**
   A. He tells George that he understands.
   B. He says that it was inevitable.
   C. He laments the loss of a noble man.
   D. He wonders why George is so upset.

10. **Why does George shoot Lennie?**
   A. He shoots Lennie because he does not care whether Lennie lives or dies.
   B. He murders Lennie to give him a more merciful death than he would suffer from Curley.
   C. He sacrifices Lennie to save himself.
   D. He murders Lennie because Lennie attacks him.

11. **What does George tell Lennie before he shoots him?**
   A. He says that he has to do this for Lennie's own good.
   B. He tells Lennie that he will have his rabbits soon.
   C. He apologizes to Lennie.
   D. He tells Lennie that he could live easily without him.

12. **Which of the following best describes Steinbeck's portrayal of Aunt Clara as Lennie imagines her.**
   A. She is a kind old woman who consoles Lennie.
   B. She is a young woman much like Curley's wife.
   C. She is a shrewish lady who criticizes Lennie.
   D. She is a cold and distant woman who says little.

13. **Which of the following characters is not paired with his appropriate job at the ranch?**
   A. Candy - swamper
   B. Carlson - ranch manager
   C. Slim - jerkline skinner
   D. Crooks - stable buck

14. **What does Candy think that Curley plans to do when he finds Lennie?**
   A. lynch him
   B. shoot him
   C. try him for murder
   D. strangle him

15. **Why did George stop playing tricks on Lennie?**
   A. He came to pity Lennie.
   B. He realized that Lennie would do whatever he said.
   C. He realized that Lennie might eventually retaliate and hurt him.
   D. Aunt Clara reprimanded him.

16. **Of Mice and Men takes place near what city?**
   A. Soledad
   B. Salinas
   C. California
   D. Sacramento

17. **Which of the following animals does Lennie not kill in the novel?**
   A. a human
   B. a mouse
   C. a puppy
   D. a rabbit

18. **What was Lennie's dream job on the farm that he plans to start with George?**
   A. He was to have tended rabbits.
   B. He was to have tended chickens.
   C. He was to have cared for the vegetable garden.
   D. He was to have kept the place clean.

19. **Curley's wife is named _____.**
   A. We never learn.
   B. Eve.
   C. Suzy.
   D. Clara.

20. **What is Candy's dog's name?**
   A. We never learn.
   B. Lulu.
   C. Sheep.
   D. Rover.

21. **What is Slim's dog's name?**
   A. We never learn.
   B. Red.
   C. Lulu.
   D. Sheep.

22. **Who wears a glove full of vaseline?**
   A. George
   B. Curley
   C. Carlson
   D. Candy

23. **What is the point of wearing the vaseline-filled glove?**
   A. We never learn.
   B. To allow the glove to fit.
   C. To help recover from a burn.
   D. To keep one hand soft.

24. **Who is described: "He was a jerkline skinner, the prince of the ranch."**
   A. Curley
   B. Carlson
   C. The boss
   D. Slim

25. **Which of the following characters is black?**

A. Lennie
B. Crooks
C. Slim
D. Candy

Quiz 2 Answer Key

1. **(A)** He does not have to commit to a prostitute.
2. **(B)** She threatens to have Crooks lynched.
3. **(D)** He says that George might leave Lennie.
4. **(C)** He bounces the puppy too hard.
5. **(A)** He becomes angry at the puppy.
6. **(B)** She wanted companionship.
7. **(C)** He worries that this will upset their plans to get a place together.
8. **(B)** He finds a rabbit.
9. **(D)** He wonders why George is so upset.
10. **(B)** He murders Lennie to give him a more merciful death than he would suffer from Curley.
11. **(D)** He tells Lennie that he could live easily without him.
12. **(C)** She is a shrewish lady who criticizes Lennie.
13. **(B)** Carlson - ranch manager
14. **(A)** lynch him
15. **(B)** He realized that Lennie would do whatever he said.
16. **(A)** Soledad
17. **(D)** a rabbit
18. **(A)** He was to have tended rabbits.
19. **(A)** We never learn.
20. **(A)** We never learn.
21. **(C)** Lulu.
22. **(B)** Curley
23. **(D)** To keep one hand soft.
24. **(D)** Slim
25. **(B)** Crooks

Quiz 3

1. **Lennie hallucinates _______.**
   A. George.
   B. his Aunt Clara.
   C. a giant rabbit.
   D. his Aunt Clara and a giant rabbit.

2. **Curley's wife says that she could have been _____.**
   A. a famous singer.
   B. a rich woman.
   C. a happy wife.
   D. a movie star.

3. **What is Curley's wife wearing at the time of her death?**
   A. A red dress.
   B. A blue dress.
   C. A black dress.
   D. A white dress.

4. **What kind of feathers does Curley's wife wear?**
   A. Parrot.
   B. Peacock.
   C. Ostrich.
   D. She doesn't wear feathers.

5. **What game do the men on the farm play?**
   A. Shuffleboard.
   B. Boche ball.
   C. Backgammon.
   D. Horse shoes.

6. **What card game do the men play?**
   A. Euchre
   B. Blackjack
   C. Poker
   D. Bridge

7. **Which of the following words is not used to describe Curley's wife?**
   A. A tramp.
   B. A whore.
   C. A looloo.
   D. A tart.

8. **Crooks rubs his back with ______.**
   A. lotion.
   B. vaseline.
   C. liniment.
   D. sand.

9. **Which of the following characters is not physically injured or disabled?**
   A. Lennie.
   B. Crooks.
   C. Curley.
   D. Candy.

10. **Lennie threatens to live in a cave like a ____.**
    A. rabbit.
    B. caveman.
    C. bear.
    D. wolf.

11. **Who kills Candy's dog?**
    A. George.
    B. Curley.
    C. Carlson.
    D. Candy.

12. **What is Slim's position on the question of whether Candy's dog should live?**
    A. He says that Candy's dog should move out of the bunk house.
    B. He says that Carlson should leave Candy's dog alone.
    C. He says that Candy's dog should be shot.
    D. He doesn't offer an opinion.

13. **How many times does the boss appear in the novel?**
   A. one
   B. two
   C. zero
   D. three

14. **What color is the girl's dress in Weed?**
   A. red
   B. blue
   C. green
   D. white

15. **How did Lennie and George hide from the mob in Weed?**
   A. They hid up to their necks in water.
   B. They hid in a barn loft.
   C. They hid in the bushes.
   D. They hid in a bale of hay.

16. **Did Lennie intend to rape the girl in Weed?**
   A. No.
   B. George isn't sure.
   C. Yes.
   D. George doesn't say.

17. **Who says the following: "I don't like mean little guys."**
   A. George.
   B. Lennie.
   C. Curley.
   D. Candy.

18. **To whom does the above quotation refer?**
   A. Lennie.
   B. Curley.
   C. Carlson.
   D. Candy.

19. **What kind of gun does Carlson have?**
   A. A shotgun.
   B. A Smith and Wessen.
   C. A Luger.
   D. A six-shooter.

20. **What is a "goo-goo"?**
   A. A non-white person.
   B. A policeman.
   C. A goody-goody.
   D. A loose woman.

21. **Who of the following does not enter Crooks' room in Chapter Four?**
   A. Lennie
   B. Slim
   C. Candy
   D. Curley's wife

22. **At the end of Chapter Four, Candy's wife threatens to do what?**
   A. To accuse Crooks of attempting to rape her.
   B. To tell her husband that the men were hitting on her.
   C. To pit her husband against Lennie.
   D. To accuse Candy of attempting to rape her.

23. **What is Candy's wife's nickname for Lennie?**
   A. Machine
   B. Mountain
   C. Strongman
   D. Rabbit

24. **Which of the following places is a brothel?**
   A. Pearl's
   B. Connie's
   C. Eve's
   D. Susy's

25. **Who gives Lennie a puppy?**

A. George
B. Curley
C. Carlson
D. Slim

Quiz 3 Answer Key

1. **(D)** his Aunt Clara and a giant rabbit.
2. **(D)** a movie star.
3. **(A)** A red dress.
4. **(C)** Ostrich.
5. **(D)** Horse shoes.
6. **(A)** Euchre
7. **(B)** A whore.
8. **(C)** liniment.
9. **(A)** Lennie.
10. **(C)** bear.
11. **(C)** Carlson.
12. **(C)** He says that Candy's dog should be shot.
13. **(A)** one
14. **(A)** red
15. **(A)** They hid up to their necks in water.
16. **(A)** No.
17. **(A)** George.
18. **(B)** Curley.
19. **(C)** A Luger.
20. **(C)** A goody-goody.
21. **(B)** Slim
22. **(A)** To accuse Crooks of attempting to rape her.
23. **(A)** Machine
24. **(D)** Susy's
25. **(D)** Slim

Quiz 4

1. **Who of the following understands Lennie?**
   A. Curley
   B. Carlson
   C. Slim
   D. Candy

2. **Who is a swamper?**
   A. Lennie
   B. Crooks
   C. Carlson
   D. Candy

3. **Who is a skinner?**
   A. George
   B. Lennie
   C. Carlson
   D. Slim

4. **What does a skinner do?**
   A. Skins the game.
   B. Drives the mules.
   C. Works the hay baler.
   D. Runs the farm.

5. **At the beginning of Chapter Six, a ____ swallows a _____.**
   A. fox...rabbit.
   B. bear...salmon.
   C. heron...snake.
   D. snake...mouse.

6. **Why does Lennie return to the bushes at the beginning of Chapter Six?**
   A. Because he wants to pet the dead mouse.
   B. Because he always retraces his steps.
   C. Because George told him to if there was trouble.
   D. Because he gets lost.

7. **Who shoots Lennie?**
   A. George
   B. Carlson
   C. Lennie himself
   D. Slim

8. **Whose gun does Lennie die by?**
   A. George's
   B. Lennie's
   C. Carlson's
   D. Slim's

9. **When Lennie hallucinates, he imagine's Aunt Clara speaking in ____ voice.**
   A. her own
   B. his own
   C. George's
   D. Slim's

10. **Lennie imagines the giant rabbit speaking in _____ voice.**
    A. Candy's
    B. his own
    C. George's
    D. Slim's

11. **How many times does Lennie hear "about the rabbits"?**
    A. One
    B. Two
    C. Four
    D. Three

12. **Who is the deputy sherrif?**
    A. Al Wilts
    B. Bill Tenner
    C. Bill Johnson
    D. Whit Jackson

13. **What river does the novel open and close beside?**
   - A. Salinas
   - B. Colorado
   - C. Los Angeles
   - D. Mississippi

14. **Who does Lennie intentionally injure in the book?**
   - A. Curley
   - B. The mouse
   - C. The puppy
   - D. Curley's wife

15. **Who says the following: "Why do you got to get killed? You ain't so little as mice."**
   - A. George
   - B. Lennie
   - C. Slim
   - D. Candy

16. **After he kills his puppy, Lennie does what?**
   - A. Hides it in his pocket.
   - B. Throws it into a river.
   - C. Throws it out the window.
   - D. Buries it in the hay.

17. **Where are the puppies?**
   - A. In Candy's room.
   - B. We never learn.
   - C. In the bunk house.
   - D. In the barn.

18. **Who does George talk with at the end of the novel?**
   - A. Curley
   - B. Carlson
   - C. Slim
   - D. Candy

19. **Who does Curley talk with at the end of the novel?**
   A. George
   B. Carlson
   C. The boss
   D. Slim

20. **Of Mice and Men was first published in what year?**
   A. 1930
   B. 1937
   C. 1940
   D. 1947

21. **What novel did Steinbeck publish after Of Mice and Men?**
   A. The Winter of Our Discontent
   B. Cup of Gold
   C. East of Eden
   D. The Grapes of Wrath

22. **Who directed the first staging of Of Mice and Men on Broadway?**
   A. William Wyler
   B. George Kaufman
   C. John Steinbeck
   D. George M. Cohan

23. **Which of the following books was NOT written by Steinbeck?**
   A. Tortilla Flat
   B. The Bridge of San Luis Rey
   C. In Dubious Battle
   D. Cannery Row

24. **Steinbeck was born and raised where?**
   A. Topeka, Kansas
   B. Northern California
   C. New York, New York
   D. Salinas Valley, California

25. **John Steinbeck won the Nobel Prize in what year?**

A. 1937
B. 1940
C. 1947
D. 1962

Quiz 4 Answer Key

1. **(C)** Slim
2. **(D)** Candy
3. **(D)** Slim
4. **(B)** Drives the mules.
5. **(C)** heron...snake.
6. **(C)** Because George told him to if there was trouble.
7. **(A)** George
8. **(C)** Carlson's
9. **(B)** his own
10. **(B)** his own
11. **(D)** Three
12. **(A)** Al Wilts
13. **(A)** Salinas
14. **(A)** Curley
15. **(B)** Lennie
16. **(D)** Buries it in the hay.
17. **(D)** In the barn.
18. **(C)** Slim
19. **(B)** Carlson
20. **(B)** 1937
21. **(D)** The Grapes of Wrath
22. **(B)** George Kaufman
23. **(B)** The Bridge of San Luis Rey
24. **(D)** Salinas Valley, California
25. **(D)** 1962

Made in the USA
Lexington, KY
15 August 2011